Get Me to ZERO™

Use the 2019 I.R.S. Tax Code to Pay as Little as ZERO Income Taxes During Retirement and Have a Better Life

Written By: **Mark J. Orr, CFP® RICP®**

Certified Financial Planner™

Retirement Income Certified Professional®

To be notified of the upcoming online course
of the material contained in this book
and join my email list, simply go to the website below and register.

www.SmartFinancialPlanning.com

Author of:
"Retirement Income Planning: The Baby-Boomer's 2019
Guide to Maximize Your Income and Make it Last"
"Social Security Income Planning: 2019 Baby-Boomer's Guide"

Instagram: @getmetozero   facebook.com/get-me-to-zero

1

Preface

Get Me to ZERO™ describes a path to legally pay as little as zero federal income taxes during retirement, using no tax strategy that even remotely pushes the envelope. There are seven synergistic tax strategies that take advantage of rock-solid, audit-proof sections of the IRS tax code that have been in place for decades. Anything with the name ROTH in it (ROTH conversions and both ROTH IRA and ROTH 401K contributions) are two very important parts of Get Me to ZERO™ planning. But they do come with some unwelcome IRS limitations. So, we'll also focus on one powerful strategy without those limitations that can help those who don't qualify for ROTHs.

The U.S. tax code is crystal clear in that you are legally obligated to pay income tax just one time on your income. By shifting and accumulating your savings from "forever-taxed" money into "never-again-taxed" money, business owners and hard-working, successful Americans can position themselves into the lowest retirement income tax rates – and possibly pay ZERO income taxes.

The readers that will appreciate this information the most are those, that – despite the Trump "tax cuts" – believe that federal income taxes might have to double in the next 15-25 years. There is historical precedence for this. The top marginal tax brackets have been as high as 94% and were at 70% as recently as the 1970's.

The U.S. government has made some $100 Trillion in unfunded promises (including almost $22 Trillion of debt, Medicare, Medicaid and Social Security, etc.). If income taxes go up by only 1%, the tax-saving strategies herein will have proven to be worthwhile. And even a 5% rise will be a home run for those that implement them.

Thank you for purchasing this book.
Up to $1,000/year of royalties from this book will be donated to The Rotary Foundation

Table of Contents

Introduction

This book is not going to be for everyone. It's too different. You won't read about using a combination of these seven tax strategies in mass-market publications. Too few advisors use a multi-strategy approach with their clients to address both taxes and risk. And the new 2018 tax laws make this book more relevant than ever!

The first part of this book will describe how to use ROTH IRA contributions (assuming your income is low enough to qualify), ROTH 401Ks (and similar plans at work)... plus ROTH conversions. The middle chapters will describe the "TRIPLE ZERO™" strategy and how to use it to complement anything with the name "ROTH" to help finish the job of paying ZERO taxes in retirement (or as low as your personal circumstances and goals allow). And do so with more flexibility. Pay the IRS less. Keep more and have a better life.

So, what is this strangely named 3rd strategy?

TRIPLE ZERO™ is a powerful retirement cash-flow and cash-reserve strategy that perfectly complements ROTH contributions and ROTH conversions. The TRIPLE ZERO™ strategy offers:

** ZERO Income Taxes EVER Due (when you play by the IRS rules)
** ZERO Stock Market Risk (ZERO % is Worst Return with Double-
                          Digit Potential Returns When the Markets Do Well)
** ZERO IRS Contribution Limits (Unlike ROTH IRAs, 401Ks, etc.)

And unlike ROTH IRAs, there are ZERO income limits to making contributions to a TRIPLE ZERO™. Even the very rich can fund them with $100,000's every year. And unlike Qualified Retirement plans (IRAs, 401Ks, TSPs, 403Bs, 457s etc.) you can access up to 90% of the cash value (private cash reserve) at any time... tax-free (as long as you follow the IRS rules). In fact, this strategy even enables your savings to potentially make returns in two places at once.

And if you die, the TRIPLE ZERO™ plan is self-completing. Your savings goal is reached by a tax-free death benefit for your loved ones. Yes, this strategy involves a specially-designed Life Insurance policy. But not just any policy will do, and it must be designed with the end goals in mind. Nearly $2 BILLION of new premium was paid-into this strategy in 2017 - an 18% increase over the prior year.

I think ROTH IRAs and ROTH 401Ks are wonderful and most everybody that "can" take advantage of them... should do so. They play a very important role in helping people get to pay ZERO income taxes in retirement years (or as close as possible). Wouldn't that be great – ZERO income taxes during retirement! Pay the IRS much less. You keep much more for yourself and have a better life.

But for most people, ROTH contributions and ROTH conversions are not going to get the full job done. Plus, with all the great things about ROTHs, they still have many limitations – which the TRIPLE ZERO™ strategy does not have to worry about.

You don't have to like life insurance at all, not one tiny bit. You just must hate paying future income taxes to the IRS more!

Working hand in hand with ROTHs and the four other strategies described at the end of the book, the TRIPLE ZERO™ strategy will, under the IRS laws and regulations that have been in place for decades, get many people to pay ZERO taxes during retirement.

For folks that plan ahead, it could also mean paying NO taxes on Social Security income (people who don't plan ahead might pay income taxes on up to 85% of their Social Security income). Originally Social Security was supposed to be forever untaxed. But since 1984 that's no longer the case - except for the poor!

What you'll read and learn about in the pages that follow is a real and proven multi-prong strategy, combining anything with the name ROTH in it, the TRIPLE ZERO™ strategy and perhaps four other tax strategies that can potentially give you a tax-free future. Plus, you'll enjoy cash reserves that you can access before retirement to make your money work harder for you during your whole lifetime. That means you have more financial flexibility.

This is no "get rich quick" scheme. Far from it. It takes financial discipline and devotion to your own future. When you finish this book, you'll know more about income taxes and retirement planning than most of the financial advisors that are peddling products to people who are just slightly less informed than the brokers/agents are. Nor is it a convoluted, untested tax scam.

You will become financially empowered and confident to control (as much as possible) your own taxation destiny and not have to reduce your current lifestyle when you retire due to taxes.

This is going to be fun. If you decide to embrace these seven concepts and planning ideas, it can transform your financial life. Slowly at first, but then in an unstoppable, compounding manner.

The sections relating to the TRIPLE ZERO™ plan will perhaps be the most powerful and flexible of all... but it's the least understood wealth accumulation strategy. It provides you access to your money now, plus 100% tax-free supplemental retirement cash-flow while simultaneously slashing the market risks to your retirement savings.

Fortune 500 companies, banks, small business owners, members of Congress and the wealthy have used similar plans for decades - even after these special types of "private supplemental retirement plans" were modified by three Congressional Acts in the 1980's.

Wall Street doesn't like the TRIPLE ZERO™ plan at all, nor have they embraced ROTH conversions (or even ROTH contributions).

Why doesn't Wall Street like ROTH conversions? Because when you convert a traditional IRA to a ROTH, income taxes get paid to the IRS and perhaps your state. That reduces the amount left that Wall Street (your broker or advisor) can make money on (fees and commissions). ROTH conversions give them a 15%-45% pay cut!

So, you can be one up on them by using as many of these multiple tax-free retirement income strategies as possible!

Before we really get started with the explanation of why you should want to seriously consider using all seven Get Me to ZERO™ tax strategies and how they all work together, let me just whet your appetite about the TRIPLE ZERO™ part of the strategy.

Since 2004, I've been absolutely convinced and passionate that the TRIPLE ZERO™ plan is a much safer, more predictable, more tax-efficient and more financially flexible way to plan for your future.

It's been one of the primary focuses of my financial planning firm – especially for clients age 25-62 who worry about rising taxes. I personally practice and genuinely believe every word -- as do 10,000's of other Americans planning for retirement. And 100% of my own money is invested in exactly this manner (the IRS says that I earn too much money to qualify to contribute to a ROTH IRA).

In addition to using all manner of ROTHs and specially-designed and maximum-funded life insurance contracts, there are another four synergistic Get Me to ZERO™ strategies that I also use in my financial planning practice. We'll discuss these other four strategies near the end of this book. They can increase the likelihood that you can pay as little as ZERO income taxes throughout your retirement.

Yes, there are plenty of good books about traditional retirement planning: investing with mutual funds, dividend-paying stocks, how much do I need to retire on, etc. But there are not so many books that focus on the big picture which includes income taxes. It's not what your savings earn in retirement – it's what you keep and get to spend after paying the IRS and maybe your state too.

This book describes a multi-strategy path to a tax-free retirement using 7 symbiotic tax-free strategies that fit both the letter and the spirit of the U.S. tax code. There are even more strategies to use.

Few other books focus on combining the TRIPLE ZERO™ strategy with ROTHs and other financial strategies to attempt to pay little or no income taxes during your retirement... while reducing your overall investment risks and getting better pre-59½ access to your cash. Yes, most folks would like to reduce their investment risk too.

Let me ask you a very important question. Are you 100% sure that you are going to have a great retirement... or do you have some doubts? Is the likely potential of rising tax rates and/or lower tax brackets/tax deductions contributing to your doubts?

I am on a personal mission to educate thousands of Americans about a little-known way to rid themselves of the confusion, fear and frustration of retirement tax-planning. Are you worried about taxes going up over the next 15-25 years due to our country's annual deficits, exploding national debt, and unfunded Social Security, Medicare, Medicaid, etc.? New social programs, wars?

This book fully explains how implementing these seven proven strategies can offer up to 25%-40% MORE spendable retirement income than traditional 401Ks, TSPs, 403Bs and IRAs.

Many Americans are looking for new and different ways to plan for retirement, with more flexibility, less risk, less volatility and much lower future taxation. Perhaps even ZERO income taxes in retirement. It's completely possible for many millions of middle and upper-class Americans to avoid taxation of their retirement income.

And the earlier one gets started in positioning their finances to do that, the better. No question about it. That's right, if you have 10-30 years before you retire, you are in a wonderful position. But for many folks, only 5-10 years can work well too.

The old traditional ways of retirement planning have not worked out very well for many current and pre-retirees. For some, it's been a complete disaster. They are still emotionally and financially stuck, afraid of taking future losses with their money (like in 2000-2002 and 2008) and are pretty confused on what to do next. But they realize that they need to do something.

So why haven't you heard about using a properly structured and maximum-funded life insurance policy along with ROTHs before to enjoy maximum tax-free retirement cash-flow and reduce risks?

This type of planning has been around for a long time – especially for Fortune 500 companies and the wealthy. Over the last five to ten years or so, it's becoming much more mainstream.

> **The highest form of ignorance is when you reject something you don't know anything about.**
> Wayne Dyer

If what "you thought to be true" about retirement planning, taxes and investing... wasn't actually true, when would you want to know about it? What's your 401K/IRA "exit" tax strategy?

Here's an insightful quote from FoxBusiness.com published on Feb 22, 2012: "The life insurance industry has the best IRS-approved retirement savings plan today—and most investors know nothing about it. This retirement savings vehicle is not a company-sponsored, pre-tax qualified, 401(k)-type plan. It's also not a ROTH. It's not an annuity or whole life."

The article continued: "Why not protect your safe, comfortable retirement against the risks we can't predict and can't afford to recover from on our own, and why not cut out the tax man in the process? These are all legal, and totally above board, established principles". In fact, they are decades old and well-established.

Ed Slott is a CPA and a nationally recognized expert on IRAs. Not only did he write a best-selling book "The Retirement Savings Time Bomb and How to Defuse It", his educational television specials can regularly be watched on Public Broadcasting Stations (PBS) across the country. He really knows his stuff.

Obviously, Mr. Slott loves all ROTHs and he is a big proponent of both ROTH contributions and conversions. But he completely understands the valuable benefits of adding a properly designed life insurance policy in planning ahead for a tax-free retirement.

In his book he writes, "I'm not a shill for the life insurance industry – I don't sell life insurance... It is important to look at life insurance... as a solution to a problem." I have the same view. A life insurance policy can be a good solution to overcome shortfalls of many other investment vehicles (including ROTHs). They are not perfect... but are another flexible financial tool to help people safely and predictably attain their financial and retirement goals.

The TRIPLE ZERO™ strategy is based on IRS Code Sections 7702 and 77(e). The income tax provisions of this supplemental retirement planning vehicle were modified by three Congressional Acts in the 1980's (TAMRA, DEFRA and TEFRA). The current tax treatment of life insurance has been in place for over 30 years now.

Maybe the ideas in this book can help you focus more clearly on solutions to any financial struggles and problems you may be facing or certainly point out potential opportunities that you didn't even realize existed – such as aiming for paying ZERO taxes during retirement. This book is all about you and your future. It's about using these seven tax-saving strategies to safely reach your full financial potential and achieving your financial and lifestyle goals.

I completely understand that retirement planning can be scary and even confusing for many people. There are so many choices, so many financial advisors, so many conflicting views and advice. But where else are you finding information about a comprehensive strategy with the stated goal of paying ZERO income taxes during your retirement by using a combination of seven strategies... while reducing your stock market risks at the same time (in the ROTHs as well as the life insurance). Is your CPA proactively discussing this?

What matters most to me is that you get exposed to some new planning ideas that may help you relax a bit and perhaps feel more confident about the coming decades and your future retirement.

Whether you are financially savvy yet or not, you will have a gut feeling about what you read here. It might help you gain confidence or leave you a bit skeptical. But I'm sure that you will learn a lot of information that you had no idea about before. It's my hope that most of you will feel uplifted and that you get real value from reading it. Either way, you will be better informed and educated.

This book is written for the masses of taxpayers that pay at least $7,000 to $65,000 a year in federal taxes now (in the 12%-24% tax brackets). If you pay six figures to the IRS today, this book is only the start of what you can accomplish. You'll want to learn more about pg. 160! Are there other ways to plan for a great retirement?

Of course. But do I believe, that when all things are considered, the TRIPLE ZERO™ strategy and ROTHs offer much more flexibility, lower risks, safer returns, higher net spendable future income and a much fuller suite of all around personal financial planning benefits throughout your life time than the traditional ways to invest and plan for retirement? I absolutely do and I'm certainly not alone.

Maybe investing in mutual funds, stocks, bonds, hedge funds, BITCOIN, ETFs, gold, options, futures, commodities, currencies, real estate, etc. has worked out well and will continue to work out well for you. If it has, that's wonderful – keep up the good work. That's where the ROTHs might best fit in. But in many cases, using ROTHs alone will not get you to pay ZERO income taxes or even close.

But if those types of investments haven't done so well for you or the people that you care about (big losses in 2000-2002 and 2008), there must be something else you are searching for, otherwise you would not have looked for and bought this book. So, if your own past retirement planning results have been disappointing or you worry about the prospect of higher taxes, this book is for you.

Shouldn't your current retirement planning include future tax planning? Do you have a tax-savvy exit strategy for your traditional retirement investments? Would having one be a smart idea?

I'm not looking to win friends in the stockbroker and good-ole-boy-based financial communities – I'm looking to inform and positively change real people's lives and save taxes. Some people are just closed-minded about anything new and won't consider anything different. That's OK. I don't mind ruffling a few feathers.

To be sure, I'm not writing about the same old retirement accumulation advice that you'll read in magazines like Money, Smart Money or Kiplinger's: work hard, live well below your means, save more, diversify and buy these 10 "five-star" mutual funds.

That's not an after-tax retirement income plan at all. That's not an overall financial strategy to live by. This book describes what I firmly believe to be the absolute best complete retirement income plan package for the 21st century... that will also serve your family well before retirement too. Yes, during your working years too!

The three main planning methods described here are not for everyone. It's for the 50% or more Americans that want a solid planning strategy that will help them save taxes in retirement and reduce their risks, regain full confidence in their future and who are willing and open to explore ideas that are new to them. They also want more financial flexibility today, access to their savings and to "sleep at night" right now and throughout their retirement.

Now NO plan is 100% risk-free because there's a world full of risks out there, but the TRIPLE ZERO™ strategy is almost impossible to beat – especially when combined with all ROTHs and the other tax strategies. There is no stock picking, market timing, portfolio allocation, guesswork or luck needed because your account can never lose money due to stock market drops. Yet you can earn up to 12%-26% (or more) a year when the market does really well.

And all those gains to your account are locked-in and protected from future market losses. Better yet, when you take money out of your account properly, it will never be taxed under current and longstanding tax laws. I'll also explain how your TRIPLE ZERO™ plan can act as your "private bank" and handle all your personal financing needs and potential cash for other investments too.

"Wealth is not how much money YOU make. It is how much money... your ASSETS make." Robert Kiyosaki

Yes, a huge advantage of the TRIPLE ZERO™ strategy is that your savings can eventually work for you in two places at the same time. And it can do so for you at favorable terms and with uninterrupted compounding. We call this our "private cash reserve" strategy (or private reserve for short). I'll get more into that later.

Even though I love ROTHs (in a later chapter I will discuss how I suggest optimizing them), you should understand that ROTHs cannot do those things for you, but they should still play a vital role in reaching the point of paying ZERO (or as little as possible) total income taxes during retirement. OK, let's get started.

The Case for Rising Income Taxes

You are probably wondering why this whole book is devoted to the goal of paying ZERO income taxes in retirement... OR owe as little as legally possible?

Well, the snapshot below that I took on December 12, 2018 of the US Debt Clock website, says it all. The number in the upper left-hand corner is the total US National debt. The number is over $21.9 TRILLION dollars. That $21.9 Trillion figure equals over $66,500 for each US citizen and more importantly over $179,000 per US taxpayer. You do know that something like 50% of the "income earning" adult Americans do not pay ANY income taxes, don't you?

14

It's true. It's the other 50% of <u>taxpayers</u> (you and I) that will have to pay the growing debt – not the number of total U.S. citizens.

That $21.9 Trillion <u>excludes</u> un-funded Social Security, Medicare and Medicaid obligations which adds another $51+ TRILLION to our nation's obligations). Then there's un-funded Federal employee pensions and other financial obligations which add TRILLIONS more.

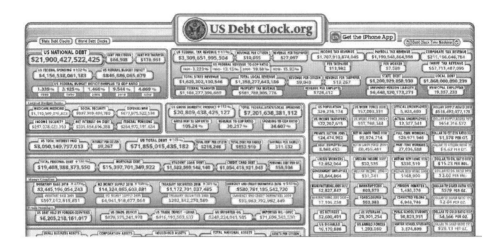

I understand that it is hard to see the numbers above, but you can see the up-to-the-second real-time numbers at any time by going to the **www.USDebtClock.org** website. It's an eye-opener.

Without getting into politics, the Federal Debt doubled during the Obama years. It also doubled during the George W. Bush years. And as Americans live longer, the unfunded liabilities of Social Security, Medicare, Medicaid, federal and military employee pensions and benefits, etc. will likely only accelerate.

Despite the recent Trump "tax cut", when I ask a room full of people at a retirement class whether they think taxes are going to be higher in the next 15-25 years... or lower, what do you think is the overwhelming response? What is your opinion? Do the facts support your opinion? I hope so.

In my own experience (and every financial colleague that I know across the country has experienced in a similar situation) the crowd says... "higher income taxes" are coming. It's simple MATH.

Now there has been a bit of excitement since the Trump "tax cuts" effective in 2018. Some folks will have a tax savings and others will pay more under the new law. But for most of my clients, it doesn't appear that there will be major reductions in actual taxes owed. However, the changes in the law will only be for an eight-year period. The new tax law expires in 2025. And a future change in Congress might make it sooner than that! We'll have to see.

But no matter what happens over the next 3, 8 or 10 years, tax rates, brackets, deductions, etc. are always in flux over time (different Presidents, Congress members, etc.) and with all the national debt and unfunded obligations, that money must come from somewhere and the odds are pretty high it's going to come from the 50% of the people that are paying taxes today. You and I.

David Walker served as United States Comptroller General and was head of the Government Accountability Office from 1998 to 2008, under Presidents Clinton and Bush. He is the author of "Comeback America" and now founder and CEO of the Comeback America Initiative. On January 11, 2010, he famously forecast on NPR radio that income tax rates would likely have to double to liquidate our nation's debt and pay for underfunded entitlement programs like Medicare, Medicaid, Social Security and others.

He understands that either taxes will have to double... or

government spending will have to be drastically cut in order to fix our country's finances for future generations. We cannot keep putting our country's "current lifestyle" by spending on the national credit card. Spending money that we don't have and putting the eventual burden of repaying it onto our children and grandchildren.

Being a former Washington insider, David Walker likely knows more about our country's true fiscal viability than anyone else, so it's important that we take his warnings seriously - like Paul Revere. It's also important that people begin preparing for the tax challenges of which he speaks so often about.

For example, if tax rates in the future are likely to be higher than they are today, why not begin to reposition your savings to tax-free vehicles like Roth IRAs, Roth 401Ks, do Roth conversions, and properly utilize life insurance along with the 4 other tax strategies?

From an April 2017 Forbes article: "With tax rates constantly changing, life insurance can also function as a hedge against future tax rate hikes. "The tax-preferential treatment of life insurance can be especially advantageous for individuals in a higher income tax bracket or as a hedge against a rising tax environment. As taxation rises, tax-free cash flow becomes more advantageous. Tapping into cash value income tax-free can be a great way to supplement a retirement income plan and, at the same time, help manage taxes."

The next chart is a history of the top income tax rates that go from 1913 to 2018. Those top tax rates go from 7% in the very early years to as high as 94%. From 1951 to 1963 the top rate was 91% on income over $400,000. In the 1970's top tax rates were 70%!

What is very interesting to me, is to have the year by year lowest and top tax rates and the respective tax brackets that the IRS used,

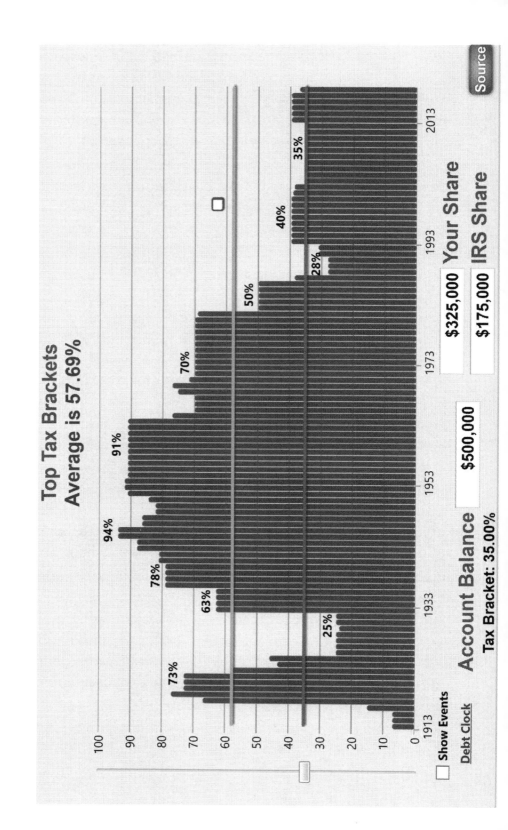

so visit: **www.smartfinancialplanning.com/matters-tax-rates-tax-brackets/** to see the year by year tax rates and tax brackets.

I'll give you a few examples of how Congress can change not only the tax rates... but the tax brackets that apply to them. As you'll see, sometimes changing the brackets is more effective in raising total income tax revenues for the IRS -- without raising tax rates!

In 1941 the lowest tax rate was 10% and the highest tax was 81% on taxable income over $5 million. Not too many folks were taxed at the 81% rate as you can imagine. But the next year, in 1942, the lowest rate was raised from 10% to 19% and the highest tax rate was increased to 88%. Huge tax increases for most Americans... with the stroke of a pen! The taxpayers had no votes or say at all.

But the 2nd BIG change that year (1942) was to the "bracket" for that highest rate. The top tax bracket was reduced from $5 million down to $200,000! That caught many more people paying that obscene 81% tax rate. Another example: in 1981 the top tax rate was 69% on taxable income over $215,000. The next year, the rate dropped down to 50%... but on all taxable income over $85,600!

Forbes contributor Mike Patton wrote in August 2013: "The more income government requires, the more taxes will have to be raised. The problem is that there are not enough "high-income earners" to satisfy today's debt and deficits. This means that middle-income Americans will soon be in the scope of the Congressional tax rifle".

..."As I have written before, a government can over-tax the rich until they are no longer rich. However, the rich will take measures to avoid this, and they can certainly afford to do so. Since the poor have nothing to tax, the middle class will be forced to ante up." Taxes must rise for some 35 million households. Yours and mine!

The combined net worth of the Forbes 400 Richest Americans List is $2.5 Trillion dollars. If the US government confiscated every dollar they had, our country would still have $19.4 Trillion of debt and other unfunded liabilities would not have been reduced at all.

There is no shortage of economists and scholars who realize that unless government spending is drastically cut, or taxes are raised significantly (or some combination of the two), that our country is on a path to bigger problems than can be realistically dealt with. But our politicians are doing little to fix these growing problems.

What if David Walker is right? Could top tax rates increase back towards 50% or more like were prevalent for over 50 years? Could Congress increase tax revenues by pushing tax brackets downward? Could the lowest bracket go from 10% to 25%? Could they reduce or eliminate deductions as they did in the new Trump tax "cuts"?

And what about state and local income taxes – are they poised to increase? As municipalities and states face bigger and bigger deficits, there will be rising pressures to raise income taxes as well. If you live in California, state income taxes recently went up another 3% to 13.3% for the wealthiest. What state will increase taxes next? Even states with no current income taxes might be forced by their fiscal problems to begin taxing their residents!

Since David Walker's prediction on NPR in 2010, the Federal Debt has almost doubled. Do you think he is more worried or less worried today about the need to raise taxes (or cut spending) than he was back then to prevent a fiscal disaster? So, with all of that in mind, does it make any sense to consider taking practical steps now to prevent potentially higher income tax bills down the road – when you can least afford it (in retirement)? Does strategic "tax diversification" and forward tax planning make sense to you?

Steps for tax diversification include looking at ROTH IRA and/or ROTH 401K contributions, ROTH conversions and taking other steps to make Social Security checks go untaxed (under current laws). We'll explore these and other planning steps in upcoming chapters. But for many people, the ROTH strategies alone won't do the trick.

So I'll explain on how using the TRIPLE ZERO™ strategy in strategic conjunction with the ROTHs (with benefits that ROTHs do not have) to reduce the impact of any tax rate/bracket changes that Congress decides to make "for us" down the road. But first, let's continue to set the stage and bust a few prevalent myths about retirement.

Busting Five Retirement Myths!

Please don't be offended if the following myths contradict what you've been taught. It's not your fault. It's what you've been told. You are probably a very bright person, so you're going to quickly catch-on, that what you were taught as the best ways to plan for a prosperous and long retirement... probably aren't. We want to make sure that you can retire... and never have to UN-retire!

Knowing the truths about these five myths will better prepare you for the retirement you dream about. So, let's look at each of these retirement "myths". If you keep an open mind, you can dramatically improve your planning for retirement with much less stress and with possibly lower fees than you are currently paying your advisor, your 401K plan or mutual fund managers. So why not get your favorite drink and enjoy this next chapter.

Myth #1: 401Ks, 403Bs, TSPs, SEPs, SIMPLEs and traditional IRA's are the best places to save for a long and prosperous retirement.

Well if these retirement savings vehicles are so great, why did Time Magazine have a cover article entitled **"Why It's Time to Retire the 401(k)"** in October 2009? (please Google it).

Here's a great one-liner from the text, "The ugly truth though, is that the 401(k) is a lousy idea, a financial flop, a rotten repository for our retirement reserves." Now Time magazine got the problem right, but they came up short in giving its readers solutions that they could actually implement back then. But they aren't financial planners, they are professional reporters who dig up the truth.

And Time Magazine isn't the only media to spotlight the short-comings of a 401K plan. Historically, most plans have some really bad and/or only a few mutual fund choices plus exorbitant annual fees that they don't tell you about (nor do you see) - sometimes as much as 2.5% per year. High fees with little added-value to you.

That's money taken off the top of your savings annually. Those lousy investment choices and high fees can shortchange your total future retirement income by up to $100,000's. High fees (without either higher performance and/or the added value of fuller, more complete financial advice) have the same negative effect on your retirement dreams as does getting lower average annual returns.

Also, Google the Bloomberg News video called "401(k) Hidden Fees" and watch it. And do the same with the CBS 60 Minutes profile called "401(k) Recession". That's a real shocker too.

"Qualified Plans" like 401Ks, 403Bs and IRAs give tax deductions now... BUT come with monster-sized landmines like getting access to your savings. And whatever "account value" that your 401K or IRA statement shows, that money is NOT ALL YOURS. A good part of it belongs to the IRS (and maybe your state too). And there are strict rules and likely penalties to getting any of your money out before you turn age 59½. You have limited access to your cash!

Either way, Uncle Sam is going to get a big share of every dollar of "your" 401K, TSP or 403B retirement cash someday – via income taxes. And you are probably paying much higher fees than you believe you're paying -- as many fees are well-hidden. I could go on, but that's just the start of their problems. Again, the media doesn't give you any answers to these huge problems, but you'll find great solutions later in this book.

Myth #2: You should contribute as much as you can to your 401K, TSP, 403B or a traditional IRA so you can take tax deductions now.

You are never SAVING TAXES in a tax-deductible retirement plan at work or in a "tax-infested" traditional IRA – you are only POSTPONING paying them to the future. And to make it worse, you are postponing paying taxes at a tax rate and bracket that has not been set by Congress yet. That's right, nobody has any idea.

Yup, that's the horrendous trap of a qualified plan – postponing and mounting future taxes. In 2019, taxable income above $39,475 if you're single or $78,950 if you're married puts you in the 22% marginal tax bracket. Then add state income taxes of 5% or so. Let's say you contribute $10,000 a year to your 401K for 30 years. In the 27% total tax bracket, you'll "save" $2,700 a year in income taxes.

Over 30 years, you will have "saved" $81,000 in taxes ($2,700 per year x 30 yrs.) on your $300,000 of total retirement contributions. Now let's fast forward to your retirement. You really did NOT save a single dime in taxes. You only postponed paying them and created a big, future taxable "time-bomb" – that will explode at a time when you can least afford it (during your retirement). Tax-deferred money = "tax-infested" money!

If you take $40,000 out of your taxable 401K/IRA in retirement and that income puts you in the same tax rate of 27%, you'll pay $10,800 in taxes on this distribution. In just your first eight years of taking income from your 401K, you will have "repaid" the IRS more than the $81,000 of your so-called "tax savings". That's exactly what you actually "saved" in taxes during the whole 30 YEARS of making annual contributions to your qualified retirement plan.

Whether you think income tax rates are going to get higher… or just stay the same -- ONLY contribute enough money to your 401K to get the "full employer match". That's free money that you should grab! But I wouldn't contribute a penny more.

After taking annual retirement income for more than those first eight years, your 401K or IRA will cost you a FORTUNE in taxes. If you live 30 years in retirement, you could pay some $330,000 in taxes on withdrawals from your 401K. That's right; you could pay as much to the IRS (and perhaps your state) in taxes as you actually contributed into your 401K retirement plan. Think about that.

Americans are NEVER saving taxes by contributing to a 401K, TSP, 403B or a traditional IRA plan. You are only postponing and dramatically increasing the total amount that you will have to eventually pay to the IRS. But "they" don't tell you about that part.

Future taxes (even if tax rates stay the same) on your retirement accounts are a real financial liability that must be paid, just like a mortgage or student debt. Plus – you are required to take annual Required Minimum Distributions (RMDs) and then pay income taxes on these annual withdrawals once you become age 70½.

And withdrawals from your 401K or any pre-tax plan may cause your Social Security checks to become taxable too. I'll explain later.

If given the choice, would a savvy farmer rather pay income taxes on the low cost of his bags of seed today, or on the much larger value of his truckloads of harvest later? It is very simple, deferred taxes equals compounded taxes. So, whose retirement are YOU planning for -- YOURS... or Uncle Sam's?

Myth #3: My income tax rates will be lower during retirement than my current rates.

You were probably told that your tax rate would be lower in retirement than it is now. Really? It's possible, but how likely?

With the National debt at nearly $22 TRILLION dollars and growing at some $3 million a minute, many people believe that taxes will go higher. Add the more than $51 TRILLION dollars in un-funded Social Security, Medicare and Medicaid promises. As written pages back, each US citizen owes over $66,500 and more importantly over $179,000 is owed by each US taxpayer.

I'm told that the new Trump tax bill will add another $1.5 Trillion to the debt. Should an infrastructure bill pass (which is badly needed) – how much will that add to our nation's debt?

In these uncertain political and the so-called *new-normal* economic times, it's a great idea to learn different wealth, investment and tax planning strategies.

Would you bet on lower taxes during retirement? Will your house be paid off when you are retired? If so, there goes your mortgage interest tax deduction. And Congress can change tax deductions at any time like they did in 2018 with $10,000 deduction limits on state and local taxes and the elimination of personal exemptions ($4,000 for each dependent)!

Don't kid yourself by thinking your tax bills will go down in retirement. Our country cannot afford your taxes to go down for long. I suggest that you pay taxes once (on your paycheck) and then never have to pay them again. Move your money from the "forever taxed" accounts to the "never taxed" accounts.

Below is a photo of what your annual Social Security statement says. They'll run out of money unless they cut benefits or increase taxes. Medicare and Medicaid are in even worse financial shape.

Again, even if you don't need the money in your "tax-postponed" qualified plan, you're required by the IRS to start taking cash out at age 70½ (Required Minimum Distributions – RMD's) - Why? Because Uncle Sam wants to finally tax you on it! Whether you want to take the money... or not. My clients hate that RMD rule.

* Your estimated benefits are based on current law. Congress has made changes to the law in the past and can do so at any time. The law governing benefit amounts may change because, by 2034, the payroll taxes collected will be enough to pay only about 77 percent of scheduled benefits.

Will the so-called "rich" even get Social Security?

But ROTHs and the fast-growing TRIPLE ZERO™ plans described later offer tax-free distributions and it never requires you to take anything out if you don't want to. You... and not the government will always be in control of your money with Get Me to ZERO™!

Myth #4: Stock market returns average about 8%-11% a year over the very long run.

Well that's true – but the myth is, that most investors actually get anywhere close to those returns in THEIR OWN portfolios.

In 2018, the highly respected research firm DALBAR, released their annual study that found that while the S&P 500 index had returned +7.2% annually over the 20-year period ending in 2017, the average equity investor -- only earned +5.29% a year over those two decades. That's a 26% lower average annual return.

It's the 25th year in a row, the "twenty-year DALBAR study"

showed that average investors do much worse than the market (the last 10-years were even worse). Average means that half of these investors did better, and half did worse.

But the average equity investor is getting better! Over the last 30 years (ending 2016), the average investor lagged the S&P 500 index return by -6.18% a year. Please Google: DALBAR study

And according to USNews.com, "A report on ETFs (Exchange Traded Funds) reached a similar conclusion. In 68 out of 79 ETFs, the returns experienced by investors lagged that of the ETFs themselves by over 4%".

Besides investors "chasing" last year's "hottest" ETFs and mutual funds and getting "hot tips" from well-meaning friends and UBER drivers, why do average investors fare so badly?

The answer is that many people can be way too emotional when it comes to their money. They tend to "Buy High and Sell Low"... instead of "Buying Low and Selling High". When the stock market is crashing, and they can't take seeing their losses any longer, they finally give in and sell when the market is low.

And when the market almost fully recovers as it always has, they finally forget the emotional pain of the last market drop and the actual dollar amount of their losses. They eventually invest again or "buy high" when the market has already substantially recovered.

Of course, you might be an "above average" investor according to DALBAR -- who actually did enjoy good annual returns and avoided the bear markets of 2000-2002 and again in 2008. But there is something called "sequence of returns" risk during your retirement to worry about as well. I'll write about that later too.

However, there are some powerful ways to take full advantage of the bulk of the proven long-term rise of the stock market -- without having to endure the nauseating up and down roller coaster ride. I'll explain more about them shortly too.

Myth #5: When you retire, you should move much more of your money into CD's, bonds and "fixed income" because stocks are too risky.

Let's be clear: Recessions notwithstanding, longevity, inflation and taxes are the larger demons to beat in retirement – not just stock market risk… unless you retire at the "wrong" time like in 2000. But that's another issue entirely (sequence of returns risk).

Now let's talk about longevity in relation to "fixed income" investments. The average lifespan of Americans has been rising for many decades and will continue to do so as medical advances keep us alive longer. A couple aged 65 today, has a joint life expectancy of age 92. That means at least one of them is likely to live that long or even longer. So, if we have a 25 to 35-year retirement income "problem" and we need a 25 to 35-year income "solution".

There are about 72,000 Americans that are 100 years or older today and that number will likely double each decade. You or your spouse could easily be one of them. Planning for a retirement income stream that lasts until age 95-100 is the only prudent thing to do, as nobody wants to outlive their savings.

Unless you are one of the few to die early, you're probably going to live a long life. The other problem you must face is inflation risk. Most folks don't think about the adverse effects of inflation on their retirement and what it will really cost them to live a similar lifestyle two to four decades from now. Will your income keep up?

Every year, everything that you need or want to buy will cost more. Let's say that you need $100,000 of annual income (in today's dollars) to provide for a similar lifestyle when you retire. How much future income will you need to live the same way?

At just 3% average inflation, you'll actually need $242,000 of annual income to live the same way 30 years from now as you do to live on $100,000 today. To be more exact, you have a huge 30 or more year "rising" income problem. Look at the inflation chart below. It shows only one year when CPI was negative (-0.4%).

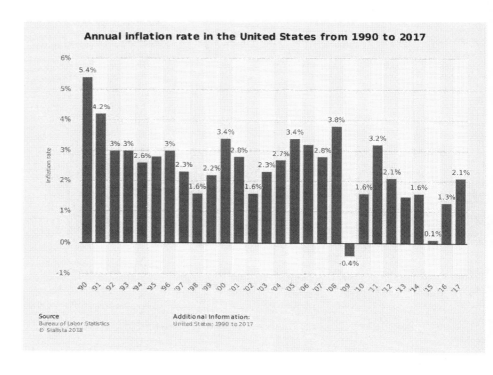

It's my personal belief as well as several prominent economists that inflation will be higher over the next few decades than it has been over the last 20 years. But let's assume it's only 3%. Looking at it another way, that $100,000 of retirement income you were hoping to enjoy 30 years from now… would only buy about $41,200 worth of "today's" goods and services at that point.

Let me ask you 2 questions. What is the name of the investment "asset class" you may have been taught that is the safest and most appropriate long-term retirement income solution, which it turns out, has never actually worked? It's called "fixed income". Heck, just the name "fixed income" tells you that it won't solve a long-term "rising income" problem. Inflation will destroy the purchasing power of money invested in traditional fixed income.

Ok, here's my second question. What class of investment assets do you probably feel is too risky as an appropriate retirement income solution, which it turns out to be the best offense to solve a "rising income" problem over a 30-year period? The answer is the stock market. It's the only place to take advantage of the consistently rising growth, profits and value of the best companies in America and the world, to trounce inflation over time.

I'll write it again. On average, at least one person in a married couple is probably going to live a long life (and then maybe only living with just one monthly Social Security check), so longevity and inflation are two of your biggest retirement risks.

So, you need to be invested more in equities and not as much in "traditional" fixed income, to produce a rising income to beat 30 or more years of inflation. I prefer non-traditional "alternatives" to bonds for the fixed income component of investment portfolios.

And staying invested in the stock market would be "easy" to do if you could only… not panic or need to continue spending your retirement savings when the market is crashing. But that's hard to do, isn't it? In fact, few people stay invested in the market when it's crashing. At one point they can't take seeing any more losses in their accounts and sell everything. But we'll discuss some solutions to harness the inflation-beating power of the stock market while capturing much of their upside as possible in upcoming chapters.

So we've now busted those five retirement myths. We've learned that 401Ks or other qualified retirement savings plans may not be the best place to save for retirement with their big market risks, fees, taxes and little early access to your cash. Plus, we've seen that "saving" a dollar in taxes today with a 401K or IRA tax deduction will only cause you to compound your total taxes owed to the IRS by perhaps four times as much during retirement. You never save taxes – you are only postponing them! Is that a tax-smart strategy?

And with our national, state and local debt, do you really think tax rates will be lower in 10-30 years -- especially after you've lost your big deductions like mortgage interest and state/local taxes?

Finally, how have your own investment returns been since 2000? What have your own investment statements looked like? Were you or your advisor able to average even 7% a year (2008-2017), when the S&P 500 actually earned 8.5% and the DALBAR studies show the average U.S. equity investor did only 4.88%? If not, you may need to change horses. And if you did well in the past, are you confident that you can do it over and over again?

Of course, few people are 100% invested in US equities. So how about the DALBAR study and "fixed-income" investors? Over that same 10-year period the average "fixed-income" investor only earned +0.48% -- when the Barclay's Aggregate Bond Index did +3.31% (and official CPI inflation was 1.64%). Pretty interesting.

The TRIPLE ZERO™ plan I'll explain in upcoming chapters did a +5.96% average annual return in one of the worst markets ever (2000-2010) – with no market risk or losses along the way. That return is 13 times better than the S&P 500 index's average annual return (including dividends) of only 0.44% during those 11 years.

Of course, during great times in the stock market, the total return of the S&P 500 will beat any place to put your money that offers the protection of no stock market risk. Lower risk, lower returns.

Over the 28-year period of 1990-2017 (great, good and ugly market years) the total return of the S&P 500 index had an average return of 9.81%, including dividends. The TRIPLE ZERO strategy had an average annual return of +7.59% and thus captured 77% of the full market performance since 1990. With no negative years at all.

And those gains in the TRIPLE ZERO™ strategy can be accessed anytime and enjoyed tax-free. It's the perfect tax planning strategy to complement to anything with the name "ROTH" in it.

Do You Understand How Income Taxes Work?

Up to now, I've spent many pages talking about the set-up to the Get Me to ZERO™ strategy. But before you can understand the seven tax strategies to get you there (or close), it makes sense for you to at least have a very good basic understanding of how the U.S. tax code works and how your income taxes are calculated.

Below you'll see the seven "marginal" tax rates under the new Trump tax law. These tax rates are the same regardless of how you file your federal income taxes (married filing jointly, filing as a single, etc.) and they are slightly lower than the marginal rates in 2017 (which were 10%, 15%, 25%, 28%, 33%, 35% and 39.7%).

Think of the next chart as a "tax cylinder" that you'll be pouring water (income) in. As you pour in your first drops of income, that falls to the bottom of the cylinder and is taxed at 10% until that tax bracket is filled up. Income poured in after that is taxed at the 12% rate until that tax bracket is filled in. The next income is taxed at

22% until that tax bracket is full. The next income is taxed at 24% and so on. Eventually all additional income is taxed at the 37% rate.

37%
35%
32%
24%
22%
12%
10%

No matter how much taxable income you have, some of it is taxed at 10%, some at 12% and so on. Even billionaires like Amazon's Jeff Bezos has a tiny bit of their income taxed at 10% (if only for a few seconds) and then at 12%, etc. For high-earners, eventually all their additional income will be taxed at the 37% rate. There is no upper-income cap to that top tax bracket.

There are two terms that are important to know. Your "marginal" tax rate is the highest rate that any of your income is taxed at. Your "effective" tax rate is the average rate at which all of your income has been taxed. It's the percentage of tax that you paid on your total taxable income.

The chart below shows you the level of income that the marginal tax brackets of the tax cylinder hold (how much taxable income puts you into the next marginal tax rate).

The new marginal rates are a bit lower than in 2017, but the tax brackets and new deduction laws "might" make your tax bill higher! Some Americans will save tax dollars and some will pay more.

Your 2019 individual income tax brackets

2019 Individual Income Tax Rates ▼	Single- Taxable Income	Married Filing Jointly - Taxable Income	Head of Household - Taxable Income
10 percent	0 to $9,700	0 to $19,400	0 to $13,850
12 percent	$9,701 to $39,475	$19,401 to $78,950	$13,851 to $52,850
22 percent	$39,476 to $84,200	$78,951 to $168,400	$52,851 to $84,200
24 percent	$84,201 to $160,725	$168,401 to $321,450	$84,201 to $160,700
32 percent	$160,726 to $204,100	$321,451 to $408,200	$160,701 to $204,100
35 percent	$204,101 to $510,300	$408,201 to $612,350	$204,101 to $510,300
37 percent	$510,301 and up	$612,351 and up	$510,301 and up

Anyway, forgetting Social Security withholding and Medicare payroll taxes for the moment, how much federal income tax would a couple having $200,000 of taxable income pay to the IRS using just the new $24,000 standard deduction (not itemizing deductions)? They would owe $30,445 to the IRS. How did we get to this figure?

If we start with 200,000 of adjusted gross income (the bottom line of page 1 on your 1040 tax form and the top line of page 2), we deduct the standard deduction amount of $24,400 for a couple filing jointly. That leaves us with $175,600 of taxable income that we're going to pour into the tax cylinder. Their marginal tax rate is 24% but not all of their income will be taxed at that rate. Most of it will not.

The first $19,400 dollars of this income is taxed at 10% = $1,940. Income from $19,401 up to $78,950 ($59,549) will be taxed at 12% which equals $7,146. Income from $78,951 up through $168,400 will be taxed at 22%. The tax on this $89,449 of income equals $19,679.

35

They have $6,999 left in their tax cylinder to be taxed at 24% ($175,600 AGI less the $168,401 tax bracket). That $7,199 taxed at 24% equals $1,728. That 24% is their marginal tax rate. But they only paid 24% taxes on their last $7,199 of taxable income.

You add up all of the taxes together and you come up with a total tax of $30,493. If you divide $30,445 by their total taxable income of 200,000 you'll find their "effective" tax rate is 15.22%. That's the actual percentage of their $200,000 Adjusted Gross Income that they actually paid taxes on.

I have not included FICA taxes that are withheld from your paycheck for Social Security of 6.2% on all earned income up to $132,900 (2019) and 1.45% for Medicare (on unlimited earned income) for an employee. Your employer pays the same amounts. If you are self-employed like me (you have no employer), you'll pay 12.4% for Social Security on the first $132,900 of earned income and 2.9% on all earned income (no ceiling). For this self-employed couple that would add $22,280 FICA taxes to the government.

Since FICA taxes are only paid on earned income, we don't have to worry about them in retirement (assuming you are not working) and therefore avoiding them does not have to be part of the Get Me to ZERO™ strategy.

Just for fun, I also calculated the tax on this couple for 2017 and I came up with $34,799 with an effective tax rate of 17.4%. So, for this couple with no kids and no itemized deductions, the Trump tax law saved them about $4,300. But this is a very imaginary couple indeed! Couples in this income range typically have 3-4 kids, a big mortgage, maybe living in a state with both high state income and property taxes and other variables could see a very different tax outcome.

There are three more tax brackets above the 24% marginal tax (32%, 35% and 37%). Tax bracket levels for single filers are generally half of those for married filing jointly – except at the 35% and 37% marginal tax rates. Then it gets to be unfair. And for Modified Adjusted Taxable Incomes (MAGI) of $200,000 for single filers and $250,000 for joint filers there is still an additional 3.8% surtax on net investment income including capital gains! So high-income earners could pay 40.8% in Federal taxes on their investment income.

And of course, there is the Alternative Minimum Tax (AMT) that may apply for single filers with as little as $71,700 and joint filers with $111,700 incomes in 2019. Another IRS GOTCHA!

How states (and municipalities) calculate their income tax is a whole different story and way beyond the scope of this book. Some states such as Florida and Texas have no state income taxes, others tax every dime of your income and do not tie it to your federal return. California tops out at 13.3% income tax. Wow!

Hopefully that explanation of how income taxes are calculated will help you better understand the full Get Me to ZERO™ strategy.

But before we fully explore the power of the ROTH, TRIPLE ZERO™ and four other strategies let's review traditional IRAs and the other widely used retirement savings plans such as 401Ks, TSPs and 403Bs.

Traditional IRAs, 401Ks, 403Bs, TSPs, etc.

Most people think that the acronym IRA stands for Individual Retirement Account. But that is not correct. According to the IRS Publication 590-A, IRA legally stands for "Individual Retirement Arrangement". This Publication says that an "IRA is a personal savings plan that gives you tax advantages for setting aside money for retirement".

An Individual Retirement Account is a trust or custodial account set up in the United States for the exclusive benefit of you or your beneficiaries. The account is created by a written document and is where your investment in your "I.R.Arrangement" is held. The document must show that the account meets all the legal requirements. But for purposes here, let's just call it what everyone else does – an Individual Retirement Account (IRA).

Anyway, I know that the focus of this book is describing a path to pay as little as ZERO income taxes in retirement, and a traditional IRA or 401K may or may not be part of that strategy.

However, I do want to correct some misinformation that a traditional IRA is deductible for everyone. First of all, in order to contribute to a deductible or non-deductible IRA, you need to have earned income (or at least one of you do if you are married and filing jointly) and be younger than 70½.

That's also not the case if you have "high income" or if you or your spouse is covered by a retirement plan at work.

According the IRS's website, "you are "covered" by an employer retirement plan for a tax year if your employer (or your spouse's employer) has a:

- Defined contribution plan (profit-sharing, 401(k), stock bonus and money purchase pension plan) and any contributions or forfeitures were allocated to your account for the plan year ending with or within the tax year;

- IRA-based plan (SEP, SARSEP or SIMPLE IRA plan) and you had an amount contributed to your IRA for the plan year that ends with or within the tax year; or

- Defined benefit plan (pension plan that pays a retirement benefit spelled out in the plan) and you are eligible to participate for the plan year ending or within the tax year."

In plain English, that means you are a "participant" in the case of an employer-sponsored plan if you received any "annual addition". So, in the case of a 401K, TSP, 403B, etc. in which the employee doesn't defer any of their own income, they could still be considered an active participant if they receive an employer contribution of any type such as a match or even a non-elective contribution. So just not contributing on behalf of yourself doesn't necessarily make the employee "inactive".

You can also check "Box 13" on the W-2 Form you receive from your employer which should contain a check in the "Retirement plan" box if you are covered. If you are still not certain, check with your (or your spouse's) employer.

With the traditional IRA, the limits on the amount you can deduct don't affect the amount you can contribute. However, you can never deduct more than you actually contribute.

If neither you or your spouse have the opportunity to contribute to a retirement plan at work (401K, TSP, 403B, etc.) then you can fully contribute and deduct a traditional IRA up to the full limits (2019) based on your age ($6,000 or $7,000 if age 50 or older). These new contribution limits are up $500 from 2018!

Of course, you can only contribute to ANY IRA if you have "earned income" from working (includes salaries, wages, tips, bonuses, or income from a business you operate). And you cannot contribute more than your earned income if you earn less than the above figures. For example, if you only earned $4,000 in a tax year, that would be your maximum contribution to an IRA.

Here's another misunderstood fact for married people. If you file a joint return and have taxable compensation, you and your spouse can BOTH contribute to your own separate IRAs – even if only one spouse has earned income.

Your total contributions to both your own IRA and your spouse's IRA may not exceed your joint taxable income or the current annual individual contribution limit on IRAs times two, whichever is less. Again, it doesn't matter which spouse earned the income.

However, "high income" can reduce the "deductibility" of your contributions if you or your spouse is covered by a retirement plan at work, such as a 401K. The charts below indicate the reductions in the deductibility if that is the case. They show the income limits above which all, or part, of your traditional IRA contribution won't be tax-deductible.

If YOU participate (definition above) in your employer's plan at work, here are the adjusted gross income (AGI) limitations for the traditional IRA deduction in 2019.

You'll notice that the tax deductibility of a traditional IRA is phased out (reduced) if your adjusted gross income is between $64,000 and $74,000 if you file as a single person or $103,000 to $123,000 if you file jointly and are an active participant in a plan at work. And beware of being married and filing separately – the income limitations shown below are tiny.

There is a small increase in the amounts from 2018 to 2019.

Tax year	Single filer who is an active participant	Married couple		IRA owner NOT an active participant, but spouse is an active participant
		IRA owner is an active participant		
		Married, filing jointly	Married, filing separately	
2018	$63,000–73,000	$101,000–121,000	$0–10,000	$189,000–199,000
2019	$64,000–74,000	$103,000–123,000	$0–10,000	$193,000–203,000

However, if your SPOUSE participates in an employer plan but you don't, then these higher income limits (far right) apply.

Tax year	Single filer who is an active participant	Married couple		IRA owner NOT an active participant, but spouse is an active participant
		IRA owner is an active participant		
		Married, filing jointly	Married, filing separately	
2018	$63,000–73,000	$101,000–121,000	$0–10,000	$189,000–199,000
2019	$64,000–74,000	$103,000–123,000	$0–10,000	$193,000–203,000

The charts above don't show limits to your making contribution to a traditional IRA – only the deductibility from your current taxes. Any reduction in deductibility means that you'll be making a non-deductible IRA contribution with after-tax dollars.

The after-tax money you put into a traditional IRA (your basis) doesn't get taxed when you withdraw it in retirement, but every dime of the earnings on that money is subject to future taxation.

If you are going to be eventually taxed on the earnings of a non-deductible IRA, why not make a contribution to a ROTH IRA instead. The contribution limits of to a ROTH are the same as for the traditional IRA – and you won't ever be taxed on the earnings!

Many people ask me if they need to file a form with the IRS if they contribute to a traditional or ROTH IRA. You do not -- UNLESS you make nondeductible contributions to your traditional IRA. In that case, you must file Form 8606.

Now 401K, TSP, 403B and similar retirement plans at work have no income limits. No matter what your income is (no limits), you can fully contribute to your plan at work in 2019 (up to $19,000 for ages 49 and under and $25,000 for ages 50 and older). But just like a traditional IRA, you cannot contribute more than you earn from wages, commissions and so on.

There are a few things that I really like about a retirement plan at work like a 401K. First of all, it's a savings plan that you don't have to think about. Your contributions are taken right off the top of your paycheck and placed in your account. You don't have to force yourself to make a separate transaction. It's in your retirement account before you can spend it elsewhere. For most people that in and of itself is a fantastic way to save for your future.

The other aspect of these payroll-based plans is that in many cases, you get a match from your employer! That's free money and you should take full advantage of it. At least contribute enough to your own retirement plan to get the FULL employer match.

One of the downsides (beyond being tax-infested) of a traditional IRA and traditional payroll-based plans at work is limited access to your savings if you ever need it. Any "early" withdrawals from a traditional IRA (401K, etc.) will be fully taxed plus a 10% penalty will apply (unless you're 59½ or meet another qualifying condition).

Now, the IRS allows "loans" from your 401K, 403B and TSP plan (assuming your employer's plan documents allow it) but this money should be a last resort for emergencies only. The IRS sets the maximum amount you can borrow from your 401K. It is either $50,000 or 50% of your account balance - whichever is lower.

Taking the loan has no tax consequences, assuming you pay it back under the terms. Where some folks run into tax issues, however, is if they don't pay it back. If you leave your job, even for reasons that are totally out of your control, the entire balance becomes due shortly thereafter, usually within a month or two.

In most cases, 401K loans must be repaid within five years, and the payments must be substantially equal. For example, you couldn't repay a tiny amount of your 401K loan for the first two years and then make much larger payments over the last three to meet the repayment deadline. However, the IRS does let you take a longer time to repay a loan if it's used for buying your primary home. If you need a 401K loan for a down payment on your primary residence, you can take longer than five years to pay it back.

If you don't fully repay the loan, it is deemed a distribution of the outstanding balance of the loan and it becomes fully taxable and subject to the 10% early withdrawal penalty in most cases.

You will pay interest on the loan from your 401K plan even though you're essentially borrowing your own money. The interest rate typically is slightly higher than the prime rate, and it goes back into your own account.

However, the outstanding loan balance isn't invested in the markets, so you miss out on any potential gains. For example, if you have a $25,000 loan outstanding and pay 4.5% interest, but the market increases 9 percent, you're not earning as much as you would have if you'd left the money growing in the account.

And keep in mind that you are using after-tax income to repay the loan and replace your pre-tax 401K savings. Think about that for a moment. You are going to repay your loan with after-tax dollars (putting money back in your 401K) – and then pay income taxes again on those same dollars when you take withdrawals during retirement.

There is no tax deduction on loan repayments to your 401K, TSP, 403B, etc. This is not smart and should be carefully considered!

Finally, another negative of traditional IRAs and tax-postponed plans at work is having to take taxable Required Minimum Distributions (RMDs) at age 70½. These plans may also cause your Social Security checks to be taxed. These two issues will be fully discussed later in the book. But they are more IRS "gotchas"!

ROTH Contributions -- Strategy #1

Let's start with ROTH IRAs – Get Me to ZERO™ strategy #1. I get asked what does "ROTH" stand for, like it's an acronym (R.O.T.H.). Here's its history according to Wikipedia: "Originally called an "IRA Plus", the idea was first proposed by Senator Bob Packwood (Oregon) and Senator William Roth (Delaware) back in 1989.

The Packwood–Roth plan allowed individuals to invest up to $2,000 in an account with no immediate tax deductions, but the earnings could later be withdrawn tax-free at retirement.

The ROTH IRA was actually established by the Taxpayer Relief Act of 1997 (Public Law 105-34) and named for its chief legislative sponsor, Sen. William Roth of Delaware." So, the ROTH IRA is about 21 years old. But it's not the oldest Get Me to ZERO™ strategy.

Over the years, the non-deductible contribution limits of a ROTH have increased from the initial $2,000 up to $7,000 per person today (for folks 50 or older) and only $6,000 for those younger.

Like everything else in this world, there are pros and cons to a ROTH IRA (as well as traditional IRAs). But the decision that people who are thinking about making a contribution for their retirement savings are most often concerned with is "do I take a tax deduction today with a traditional IRA… or get no tax deduction for a ROTH"?

With the traditional IRA, you get a tax deduction today but you'll pay taxes on every nickel of withdrawals (tax time-bomb). With the ROTH IRA, you will not get a tax deduction today, but you'll never pay taxes on this account (if you follow the rules). Which is better?

Of course, if the decision was just based on having a deduction today or not, the deductible traditional IRA would win every time. But there's the other half of the tax equation to consider.

With the ROTH, your future income would be tax-free (assuming you follow the rules), while every penny of your withdrawals from a traditional IRA would be taxable. Taxable at unknown future tax rates and tax brackets to be determined by Congress at any time.

Although there are other considerations in making the "should I choose" a ROTH or traditional IRA contribution decision, the biggest one for most folks is whether they are going to pay taxes at a higher rate in the future than their current tax rate. Of course, that assumes you even qualify for a ROTH contribution based on your income (see the chart below).

Most people that I speak with believe that despite the recent Trump tax cuts (which only last until 2025), with nearly $22 Trillion in debt, plus the $51 Trillion of promises made for Social Security, Medicare, Medicaid, etc., etc. that taxes will have to be higher for nearly everyone in the future. I believe that. Do you?

So, if you think your taxes, will be lower 20-30 years from now, then take the tax deduction today and pay taxes at a lower rate in the future. But if you think taxes will be higher in the future, then forgo the tax deduction now and get tax-free income when you need it most – during retirement. This is a decision that can take money from the forever-taxed bucket to the never-taxed bucket.

Paying higher taxes later means you'll likely run out of money 4-8 years sooner since you need to take more money out of your traditional IRA to have the <u>same</u> after-tax income as from a ROTH. The more the IRS gets, the less you have to spend and enjoy on your retirement lifestyle. And the faster your savings can run out.

It's not the amount of your pre-tax income that counts. The only thing that matters is your after-tax income! What you can spend.

Below is a chart of the 2018 and 2019 income limits to make a contribution to a ROTH IRA (you can contribute up to $6,000 or $7,000, depending on your age for 2019) subject to the income test. Find your tax-filing status, then if your Adjusted Gross Income (AGI) is less than $122,000 or $193,000 (filing as a Single or Jointly respectively) then you can make the full ROTH contribution.

If your AGI falls between the two limits shown in the middle and right columns, you can only make a partial contribution. And if your AGI exceeds the phase-out limit for your tax-filing status, you cannot contribute directly to a ROTH IRA for 2019.

Myself and many of my clients fall into the category of not being able to contribute to a ROTH due to our income exceeding the right column. And quite frankly, a $7,000 maximum annual contribution is not going to give folks in this income level the type of retirement lifestyle they'll be hoping for in any case.

| Tax year | Single filer | Married couple | |
		Married, filing jointly	Married, filing separately
2018	$120,000–135,000	$189,000–199,000	$0–10,000
2019	$122,000–137,000	$193,000–203,000	$0–10,000

However, there is a "back-door" ROTH IRA strategy that can be helpful for those of us to get-around the ROTH income limits. It doesn't change the issue of the relatively small annual contribution limits, but it will reap all the tax benefits of the ROTH IRA.

Very simply, you contribute to a non-deductible IRA and then convert it to a ROTH IRA. Technically this strategy is not a ROTH contribution but a ROTH conversion (which will be discussed later).

In the recent past, some financial advisors worried that the IRS would disallow this strategy, but according to Ed Slott, CPA this looks less likely after the Trump tax changes.

He says: "although it's not specifically part of the Tax Cuts and Jobs Act... several references in a conference report confirms the use of this strategy" including this one: "Although an individual with AGI exceeding certain limits is not permitted to make a contribution directly to a ROTH IRA, the individual can make a contribution to a traditional IRA and then convert it to a ROTH".

So if your income is the only point that would otherwise not allow you to contribute to a ROTH IRA, here's how you can do it. IF... you do not have any other IRAs (including SEPs and SIMPLEs), this is pretty straightforward. But it gets a bit more complicated if you do have other tax-postponed IRAs. Plans like 401Ks, etc. are not counted as an IRA and avoid these potential complications.

You see for conversion purposes, the IRS considers all your IRAs together and they are treated as one gigantic IRA account. Because all your IRAs are treated as one single account, you generally cannot segregate the after-tax contributions. Under the pro-rata rule, any conversion done from any IRA account will be deemed to consist of both some pre-tax funds and some after-tax funds.

Here's an example. You have three IRAs; one has $53,500 in contributions and earnings, one is a SIMPLE IRA with a balance of $40,000, and you just made a "back-door" contribution and want to immediately convert $6,500 in after-tax contributions.

For income tax purposes, the IRS looks at this as having one single $100,000 IRA and the $6,500 back-door conversion is considered to come out of that one single IRA.

So under the pro-rata rule, your aggregated IRA account has a balance of $100,000 ($53,500 + $40,000 + $6,500 = $100,000). Since 6.5% of your total balance is after-tax funds, any distribution you take will be 6.5% tax-free and 93.5% taxable. So you'll owe a conversion income tax on $6,077.50 ($6500 x .0935%) at your marginal tax rate to get to this money into your ROTH.

The rules get a little more complicated when converting 401K money in the same year but that is beyond the scope of this book. Please see a tax professional for more information and advice.

And just so you know, your ROTH conversion and the pro-rata calculation are both reported on IRS Form 8606 and must be filed along with your income tax return in the year of conversion.

Also, because the back-door strategy is not a contribution but a conversion. If you are under age 59½ you must wait for 5 years to have penalty-free access to the money (where your contributions to a ROTH are accessible immediately without penalty at any age).

Anyway, let's further examine the decision to contribute to a traditional IRA or the ROTH IRA next. Which is best?

Let's look at an example.

Joe and Bob are twin brothers who are age 50 and they both plan on retiring at age 70. They each plan to contribute the maximum of $7,000 into an IRA. Both are in the marginal 22% federal tax bracket now (we are ignoring potential state income taxes). Neither one wants to alter their current lifestyle. Joe wants and qualifies for the tax deduction now, so he contributes $7,000 to a traditional IRA.

Bob thinks taxes will definitely be higher at that point, so he wants a ROTH. But because he won't get a tax deduction today, he'll only put in $5,460 since he'll have to pay 22% taxes ($1,540). Which brother will have more spendable money at age 70 if they each earn 7% returns until retirement?

Well, Bob will have an account value of $223,835 in his ROTH. This amount will never be taxed. It's 100% his to spend and enjoy. But Joe will have $286,968 in his traditional IRA. It appears at first glance that Joe made a wiser decision. But did he?

You see, Joe doesn't really own that full amount and can't spend it all. He has a partner named the IRS. His IRA is bursting with unpaid income taxes. Assuming Joe's taxes are still at 22%, after paying taxes, he'll be left with the same amount of spendable dollars as Bob - $223,835 ($286,968 less 22% tax = $223,835).

Assuming tax rates for Joe and Bob stay the same, there is no difference in the amount of after-tax dollars that each has – even though Bob contributed less each year (after paying taxes upfront).

I've already addressed what I believe is a myth: that going forward, for most readers of this book, that taxes will be lower in the future. Right now, the lowest tax bracket is 10%. Back in the 1960's it was 25%. So, there is historical precedence for even folks with low incomes to pay taxes at a higher rate than today.

If tax rates for them went up by just 1%, then Bob would have made the wiser decision by electing the ROTH. But again, present and future tax rates/brackets/deductions are just one part of deciding whether to contribute to traditional IRA or a ROTH. Let's talk about some other considerations next.

Another advantage of a ROTH IRA is that direct contributions (your principal) may be withdrawn tax and penalty-free at any time. Earnings on the ROTH IRA account may be withdrawn tax and penalty-free after 5 years and once you reach age 59½ (or a certain other qualifying condition) is also met.

By contrast, any withdrawals from a traditional IRA will be fully taxed plus a 10% penalty will apply (unless you're 59½ or meet another qualifying condition). So, there is better access to your cash in a ROTH than a traditional IRA (although it is not meant to be a checkbook). I think better access is another item that tips the balance to the ROTH – especially for those well under age 50.

So, another advantage of the ROTH is distributions from it during retirement will not cause your Social Security checks to be taxed.

Whereas withdrawals from a traditional IRA (401K, 403B, etc.) are part of the "provisional income" formula that the IRS uses to determine how much of your Social Security income will be taxed.

Many people do not think that their Social Security checks will be subject to taxation by the IRS. For the poor, that is true.

But in 1984, in an effort to "save Social Security" the first time around, Ronald Reagan and Tip O'Neil came up with a tax on Social Security income that was based on one's "provisional income". For most readers, this will be the first time they've ever heard of provisional income or seen anything like the next chart!

Taxation of Social Security benefits

Taxation was instituted in 1983 and this chart has NOT changed since 1994!!

Your Filing Status	Provisional Income*	Amount of Social Security benefits that are subject to any taxation (I.R.S.)
Married filing jointly	Under $32,000	0%
	$32,000 - $44,000	Up to 50%
	Over $44,000	Up to 85%
Single, head of household, qualifying widow(er), married filing separately and living apart from spouse	Under $25,000	0%
	$25,000 - $34,000	Up to 50%
	Over $34,000	Up to 85%
Married - filing separately and living with spouse	Over $0	85%

*Provisional income = AGI + one-half of SS benefit(s) + tax-exempt interest

What counts as provisional income? Basically, all income (earned, pensions, traditional retirement account withdrawals, RMDs, all interest (including tax-free muni bonds), dividends, capital gains... PLUS one half of your Social Security income. You add it all together and then the above chart will tell you what percentage of your Social Security income will be subject to income tax by the IRS.

If you look closely at the chart, you'll notice that the provisional income figures have not changed since 1994. Back then, fewer people paid any tax on their Social Security income. But after almost 25 years of inflation, many more people have their Social Security income subject to some tax. But everybody gets at least 15% of their Social Security income tax-free, since at the highest provisional incomes the maximum amount subject to tax is 85%.

Let's get back to ROTHs. Unlike withdrawals from traditional IRAs, withdrawals from a ROTH are NOT part of the provisional income calculation. There is not even a line on your 1040 tax form where you include ROTH distributions. They are truly tax-free.

Therefore ROTHs (anything with the name ROTH in it) are an important part of the Get Me to ZERO™ planning strategy. Not only are proper withdrawals from a ROTH tax-free, but they will not cause your Social Security income to be taxed.

There is one more major reason why, for any of my clients who qualify for a ROTH, to choose it over a traditional IRA. With a ROTH, there are NO Required Minimum Distributions (RMDs).

Unlike traditional IRAs, 401Ks, 403Bs, TSPs, once you reach 70½, you are required to take out a minimum amount of your IRA each year and pay tax on it – whether you need or want the income or not. Failure to withdraw the full RMD amount will result in a 50% penalty (in addition to the income tax due) of the underpayment.

That's a 50% penalty! The IRS isn't kidding around. After years of tax-postponement, the IRS wants to start taxing your traditional IRAs at 70½. I can't tell you how many folks hate the RMD rules and having to withdraw funds from their traditional IRA and pay taxes (while increasing their provisional income at the same time and perhaps causing more taxes on their Social Security income).

Another question that I'm frequently asked, is whether you can contribute to both a ROTH 401K, TSP, 403B... and a ROTH IRA each year. While there are participation limits and restrictions imposed (previously discussed) on both types of retirement savings plans, many people will find they are able to contribute to both. And if you can take advantage of both of these retirement savings accounts, you should probably consider doing so.

But if your payroll-based retirement plan at work offers a ROTH option, I would seriously consider forgoing the tax deduction today and get all of the above-mentioned ROTH benefits tomorrow.

ROTH 401Ks, ROTH 403Bs, ROTH TSPs, etc.

One of the problems with traditional IRAs or ROTH IRAs is the low contribution limits -- $6,000 a year if you are under age 50 and $7,000 a year if you are 50 or older.

I don't know about you, but for my higher-income clients, that low level of annual contributions is not going to provide the future retirement lifestyle they've been dreaming of.

The traditional 401K plan was introduced by Congress in 1978 so it's been around for a while. Although it was never meant to replace company pension plans, that's what has largely happened in the workforce.

According to Investopedia: "The ROTH 401(k) account was created by a provision of the Economic Growth and Tax Relief Reconciliation Act of 2001. Like all provisions of the Economic Growth and Tax Relief Reconciliation Act of 2001, the ROTH 401(k) came with an expiration date, which provided that the ability to contribute to a ROTH 401(k) would expire at the end of 2010. However, the Pension Protection Act of 2006 (PPA) made the ROTH 401(k) permanent." Thank goodness for that!!

Just like the ROTH IRA, the ROTH 401K and other payroll-based ROTH plans lets you fund your account with after-tax money. You do not get a tax deduction on your contributions to a ROTH 401K, but you will never owe taxes on distributions (if you follow the IRS rules). Participants in the TSP plan are also eligible to participate in a ROTH savings account. Many 403Bs have ROTH options too.

More and more companies are offering a ROTH 401K option. Check with your HR department and see if your employer does.

Unlike the ROTH IRA, there are no income limits on contributing to a ROTH 401K (and similar plans at work). You can make $10 million a year or more and still make your full contribution to the plan (up to $19,000 for ages 49 and under and $25,000 for ages 50 and older).

Another feature of the ROTH 401K is that you can still get the company match. However, any matching contribution the employer makes will be pre-tax (you won't owe income taxes now on this portion, but you will when taking withdrawals during retirement).

Like traditional 401Ks, there can be loan provisions in a ROTH 401K and the terms are similar. However, failure to pay back any portion of the loan attributable to earnings on your contributions then becomes taxable and subject to the 10% early withdrawal penalty in most cases if you are under the age of 59½.

Just like with the argument for taking a tax deduction with the traditional IRA vs. tax-free income later with the ROTH IRA, you could have the same argument with the traditional 401K vs. the ROTH 401K.

If you are making $10,000 pre-tax contributions now to your tax-postponed 401K, you could argue that making $10,000 after-tax contributions to the ROTH 401K would reduce your take-home pay. And you'd be correct. If you are paying the tax upfront today and making the same contribution, your net paycheck will go down.

If you are in the 28% marginal tax bracket (federal and state), you'll be pay taxes on $10,000 more income if you choose the ROTH 401K option. At 28% combined tax (22% federal and 6% state) that would cost you $2,800 a year. You'd live on $2,800 less a year. If that won't work for you, then there's an easy fix.

Simply contribute $2,800 less to the ROTH (in this example). If you contribute $7,200 to your ROTH 401K rather than the $10,000 to the traditional 401K, your net paycheck will be identical.

That's what Bob did with his ROTH IRA on page 49. And as we saw in the example of Bob and Joe, both 401K contribution choices will have the same spendable (after-tax) dollars at retirement. But if taxes go up a bit, the ROTH 401K choice will be better. Plus, distributions from it will not cause your Social Security to be taxed as well as the other ROTH benefits already discussed.

A point of caution. You at least want to make a big enough contribution to your ROTH 401K to entitle you to the full company match (which always goes into your tax-postponed account and is not taxable to you today). That's free money - so grab it.

Before we wrap up the first Get Me to ZERO™ strategy of taking full advantage by fully contributing to both ROTH IRA and ROTH payroll-based retirement plans offered at work, let me tell a quick story that should prove very helpful for anyone in the early part of their career. Think about Greg's story in terms of your adult children too. Hopefully, their careers and income will rise rapidly.

Greg is one of my personal friends and mentors. He is the son of one of the country's first Certified Financial Planners™. After graduating college Greg went to work with his mom in her financial planning business.

She advised him (and everyone else) to take full advantage of making the tax-deductible traditional IRA and 401K contributions. Sounds reasonable, doesn't it?

Well like most of us in our early careers, we were earning a fraction of what we are earning now or during the final years of our careers. Greg's income was relatively low then and that put him in the low marginal tax bracket. So, he took tax deductions which only "saved" him about 15%-20% of his contributions. But he didn't save any taxes – he only postponed paying them into the future.

Let's fast forward to today. Greg is a very successful financial planner with a thriving practice as well as a partner in a firm leading a large group of other top advisors across the country. His income puts him in the highest federal tax bracket of 37%. On top of that he lives in a high-income tax state. His total income tax marginal bracket is about 45% now. That's three times his marginal tax bracket early in his career -- because his income and wealth have grown. And he thinks his taxes will be even higher in the future.

So he saved paying a small amount of taxes a few decades ago - only to have positioned himself, by having all this financial success, to paying future income taxes at three times more.

In retrospect, his mom gave him faulty advice. But this is the same advice young folks are still getting today – contribute all you can to your plan at work or a traditional IRA and save taxes today (despite being in a relatively low tax bracket now).

I do suggest contributing all you can now too – BUT to the ROTH option since your current tax bracket is likely to be low and hopefully, your growing income will put you in a higher bracket as your career progresses. This just makes common sense.

Now there is an in-between strategy of delaying your traditional tax-deductible 401K contributions until much later in your career when your highest career income levels put you in the highest tax brackets (even without the government raising tax rates) and using ROTH strategies now while your income is relatively low. The higher the income the more valuable those tax deductions will be.

ROTH Conversions – Strategy #2

The second Get Me to ZERO™ strategy is converting your current traditional IRAs and old 401Ks, 403Bs, TSPs, etc. from a previous employer... to a ROTH IRA. Taking money from your forever-taxed accounts to never-taxed accounts.

It used to be that if you earned too much income, the IRS would not allow you to convert "pre-tax" IRAs and plans at work to a ROTH. I use the term pre-tax because you never paid taxes on this money. But you'll pay taxes someday. It's tax-postponed money.

Anyway back then, if you made more than $100,000 — and that amount applied to single taxpayers as well as married couples filing joint returns — you couldn't convert your traditional account to a ROTH at all. But that law changed in 2010. Thank goodness!

Converting your traditional IRA to a ROTH is a simple process. Converting a 401K and similar payroll-based retirement plan that you may have from an old job would follow the same simple process as the conversion from a traditional IRA.

However, converting your 401K or other plan at your <u>current</u> job to a ROTH may prove problematic unless 1) your employer plan documents allow for this within your plan or 2) you are age 59½ or older and your plan allows for "in-service withdrawals".

An in-service withdrawal would allow you to take all or part of your money from your current 401K, TSP, 403B, etc. and roll it over into an IRA. Once in the traditional IRA, you could then convert it to a ROTH IRA and have many more investment choices as well.

It's important to know that should you decide to do an in-service withdrawal, you will <u>still be able to contribute</u> to the plan at work and still get any company match you may be entitled to. By using this feature in your plan at work, you get more control over where your money is invested (rather than just having the choices in your plan at work) as well as the opportunity to convert to a ROTH IRA.

How do you get your money from forever-taxed accounts (traditional IRAs, 401Ks, etc.) to never taxed-accounts? You must pay the "toll". Just like crossing a bridge from one part of New York City to another part, you must pay a toll to get across to the other side. It's the price of admission to the world of tax-free income.

The "toll" is paying the income tax now, rather than sometime in the future. For years, I've have been saying that compared to 15-30 years in the future, taxes are "on sale now". They'll likely never be lower. But with the new Trump tax law, for some people (but not everybody) the "toll" just got a little bit cheaper – temporarily!

As I wrote in the preface, the US tax code is crystal clear in that you are only legally obligated to pay income tax just one time on your dollars. With any ROTH contribution you are contributing after-tax dollars (you paid the income tax already) and you are putting dollars in a never-to-be-taxed-again account – the ROTH.

However, with a ROTH conversion, you didn't pay taxes on those dollars that are currently sitting in your traditional IRA or 401K yet. They are tax-infested, tax-postponed accounts. So, to get those dollars inside of a ROTH, you must pay the toll. You will have to pay the tax eventually, so you might as well pay it now, at a tax rate that is known and one that is historically low.

The quickest way to get a significant sum into your tax-free accounts (ROTHs) is by converting a traditional IRA/401K to ROTH status. The conversion to a ROTH is treated as a taxable distribution from your traditional IRA/401K because you are deemed to have received a payout from the traditional account with the money then going into the new ROTH account. You will get a 1099 form reporting to the IRS that you've had a taxable distribution.

Doing a ROTH conversion before year-end will trigger a bigger federal income tax bill for this year (and maybe a bigger state income tax bill too). However, current federal and state income tax rates might be the lowest you'll see for the rest of your life.

And all of the growth in the ROTH account will never be subject to taxation again, in addition to the other benefits like better access to your savings, no RMDs at age 70½ and beyond, and distributions from any ROTH will not cause your Social Security to be taxed.

Again, if you think your personal circumstances and/or belief that tax rates will <u>not</u> be higher for everyone, will cause you to be in a lower tax bracket during retirement than you are today, then ROTH conversions would not make sense. But don't forget that in the 1960's the lowest tax bracket was 25% - not the 10% rate of today.

Of course, we must be smart about doing ROTH conversions. For most people, they will want to convert over a period of time using savvy "tax-bracket management". As much as possible, we want to be mindful of your current marginal tax rate and try to keep your conversion dollars from putting you into the next tax bracket.

When you convert tax-postponed money to tax-free (ROTH), all of that conversion money will be poured into the tax cylinder – on top of all of your taxable income, bonuses, interest and dividend income from taxable accounts (1099 income) and capital gains, etc.

The amount of your conversion will be added to all of the above income and determine what your marginal tax bracket is – and those conversion dollars will be taxed according to those brackets.

For easy reference in this "tax bracket management" discussion, I have included the 2019 tax bracket chart again here. So, you can see the taxable incomes and applicable marginal tax rates as your income rises from one tax bracket to the next.

Your 2019 individual income tax brackets

2019 Individual Income Tax Rates ▼	Single- Taxable Income	Married Filing Jointly - Taxable Income	Head of Household - Taxable Income
10 percent	0 to $9,700	0 to $19,400	0 to $13,850
12 percent	$9,701 to $39,475	$19,401 to $78,950	$13,851 to $52,850
22 percent	$39,476 to $84,200	$78,951 to $168,400	$52,851 to $84,200
24 percent	$84,201 to $160,725	$168,401 to $321,450	$84,201 to $160,700
32 percent	$160,726 to $204,100	$321,451 to $408,200	$160,701 to $204,100
35 percent	$204,101 to $510,300	$408,201 to $612,350	$204,101 to $510,300
37 percent	$510,301 and up	$612,351 and up	$510,301 and up

For example, if you are married and file jointly and your marginal income puts you at the 12% marginal tax, we probably wouldn't want to convert any more money that would push your taxable income over $78,950 and put that additional taxable income into the 22% bracket. That's a big jump in your marginal tax bracket.

So if your joint taxable income was $66,500, we'd likely only want to convert about $12,000 this year – keeping you in the 12% zone.

I'm guessing that most of the readers of this book will be in the 22% or 24% tax brackets – especially since there are many more taxpayers than in the highest tax brackets (32%, 35% and 37%). But the principles will be the same for the other tax brackets as well.

In any case, you can see that there is a lot more "room-to-move" in the five higher tax brackets than in the two lowest ones.

So if your taxable income (filing jointly) is $120,000 we could convert up to $48,000 and still keep you in the same 22% marginal tax rate. We can do more heavy lifting (converting more dollars to tax-free) because those higher tax brackets are much wider.

One could argue (and I wouldn't disagree) that since the next marginal tax rate is 24%, you'd only pay another 2% on that extra income being poured into the tax cylinder and that would give you up to another $152,000 to convert BEFORE being pushed into the 32% tax rate. The 32% tax would likely be too big of a jump.

How much to convert in any tax year will be determined by where your taxable income would be without the conversion, the likely growth of your income in coming years and how many more years do you have left to convert your tax-postponed dollars into never-taxed dollars before you retire... or tax rates go up again.

But savvy tax bracket management should definitely play an important role in your conversion strategy. Please check with your tax advisor to make sure you aren't going to make a tax mistake.

You know, as I'm writing this, I've forgotten about another benefit of all ROTHs over traditional IRAs and 401Ks, etc. It may not be as important to you as all the other benefits but I want to make sure that you are aware of it.

All ROTHs that you own at your death are inherited income tax-free by your loved-ones. Just like you, your heirs will never have to pay income taxes on this money either.

If your beneficiary is your spouse, she will never have to take RMDs and can continue to let the account grow. Or he/she can spend it all at once and never pay any income tax.

However, if your beneficiaries are anyone else - usually children or even better grandchildren - they will have to take Required Minimum Distributions (RMDs) over their life expectancy. But they will not pay taxes on any distributions – lump sums or RMDs.

Depending upon the age of the heir, they may only have to take an RMD of 2%-3% a year from the ROTH balance. If the account is growing by an average of 6% a year, their tax-free income and account balance will continue to grow for decades if they choose RMDs over taking out a lump sum (spending it) or moving it into a taxable account where they'll get 1099's every year. Keep those funds in the never-taxed ROTH zone. That's a more tax-savvy move.

Many children of my clients are in a higher tax bracket than they are, so not having to pay any taxes from inherited ROTHs are a big blessing and one that they should certainly appreciate. I would!

Anyway, now let's talk about the simple ROTH conversion process. Most major IRA custodians and brokerage firms make it very easy to convert to a ROTH. The simplest way is a direct trustee-to-trustee transfer from one financial institution to the next and tell them to make the new account a ROTH. However, if you want to keep your savings at the same firm, you can simply tell your financial institution to "re-designate" your traditional IRA as a ROTH IRA instead of opening a brand-new account.

Either way, you will be issued with a 1099 tax form which will tell the IRS that you've had a taxable event and as already discussed, you will owe taxes at your marginal tax rate.

And If you want to convert your retirement savings from an old 401K or other payroll-based plan to a ROTH IRA, make sure the money is transferred directly to the financial institution. That's very important. Why?

If your previous employer company issues the check directly to you, it must withhold 20% of the account balance for tax purposes. You'll have only sixty days to deposit all the money in your new ROTH -- including the 20% that you didn't even receive. If you miss the 60-day deadline, including any money not rolled over to a ROTH it will be subject to a 10% early withdrawal penalty if you are pre-59½. That's in addition to the income taxes you will owe on the entire amount converted. The IRS loves their GOTCHAS!

So let's discuss more about the elephant in the room of any conversion to a ROTH IRA. Again, traditional IRAs and 401Ks are tax-postponed accounts. You will have to pay taxes eventually.

Keep in mind that money left in traditional IRAs and 401Ks, etc. will continue to grow – even if you stop funding them. A $400,000 IRA with no further contributions will grow to $900,000 in just 12 years at 7%. This growth alone would cause your Social Security to be taxed when RMDs are taken with average Social Security checks!

Let's say you agree with that worry. You want to Get Me to ZERO™ or as close as possible. You want to try and avoid paying taxes on your Social Security, have no future RMDs and so on. How are you going to pay the tax bill on the ROTH conversion?

Well if you are age 59½ or older, it's so easy. Rather than write a check from your checking account or taxable brokerage account, you can pay the federal and any state tax from the IRA funds itself.

Let's say that you are in the 24% federal tax bracket (no state tax). So, if you have $55,000 left in your 24% marginal tax bracket before the ROTH conversion "distribution" would push you into the 32% tax rate, you could pay the $13,200 (at the 24% conversion tax rate) right out of the $55,000 ROTH conversion itself. You could also pay any applicable state income tax out of the IRA as well. That would certainly work and is how most of the folks age 59½ or older handle it. Your old $55,000 tax-postponed account would now be a $41,800 never-taxed again ROTH. Very cool.

According to most financial planners, a better way to pay the tax is out of your taxable money and not disturb the $55,000 value of the IRA. If you have the funds available to be able to do this (rather than use your IRA money to pay the tax) I absolutely would agree. You'll be much better off in the long run.

In either case, I think making the conversion decision, was a smart one for all of the reasons I've described so far.

However, for folks that are not age 59½ yet, there is a problem that us older folks don't have if you want to pay the tax out of the IRA... rather than from outside taxable funds. The 10% penalty!

If you aren't yet 59½ when you convert the IRA or an old 401K funds to a ROTH, the IRS will charge you a 10% penalty (on top of the income tax) for "early distribution" of your IRA funds... IF you pay the income tax out of the IRA/401K funds itself!

Even though you aren't spending the money and are keeping it in an approved IRS retirement account (a ROTH), they enforce the 10% penalty. However, if you pay the tax from an outside taxable account, then there would NOT be a pre-59½ 10% early withdrawal penalty. I'll discuss a workaround in the next chapter!

FYI: If you are converting your current 401K or other payroll-based plan to its internal ROTH 401K option (if your plan allows this) and are under age 59½, there will not be a 10% penalty!

There's a two-decade-old myth out there that it will take years for a ROTH conversion to be worthwhile and of personal financial benefit. I don't believe that is true unless you are converting to at ROTH at a higher tax rate than you'll be in throughout your 25-35 year retirement. And even if that might end up being the case, the other benefits of a ROTH may have tremendous value for you.

According to Kiplinger magazine: "But remember that the tax bill on the conversion is a bill that you (or your heirs) will have to pay someday, even if you stick with the traditional IRA. Unless switching to a ROTH pushes you into a higher tax bracket than you would be in when withdrawing taxable amounts from the traditional IRA, a conversion is "break-even financially from day one," points out James Lange, an attorney, CPA and IRA expert in Pittsburgh. All else being equal, you're ahead of the game with a ROTH starting on day two because tax-free earnings are better than tax-deferred earnings". James is a friend of mine and he knows his stuff!

A second myth might be something to be wary of if your child is applying for college aid. Reporting income on your 1040 from a ROTH conversion "could wipe out any chance your child will get college financial aid". Retirement account balances are not counted for financial aid purposes on your FAFSA form (but 529 plans are!). However, colleges do ask for your annual income tax returns when calculating how much financial aid to give your kids. And remember the conversion amount is poured into your tax cylinder to compute your marginal tax rate. On paper, you'll look like you earn more money than you really do. A ROTH conversion just shifts assets.

But financial aid administrators know about ROTH conversions, and they would likely have the leeway to ignore an income anomaly such as a ROTH conversion, that makes your income look higher than it really is. So be sure to highlight the ROTH conversion so the college financial aid office better understands your tax return.

In the unlikely event that you are covered by Medicare (at 65 or older), and want to do a ROTH conversion, there's another issue to consider. A spike in your income due to ROTH conversion income could push up your Medicare Part B (and D) premium if it knocks you into another IRMAA bracket (which determines your Part B and D Medicare monthly premiums). See the income brackets below.

The first 2019 chart (based on IRMMA income in 2017) is for Part D Premiums (Prescription Drugs) which are much smaller premiums than for Part B which is the 2nd chart. Monthly Part D per/person premiums are right below:

File individual tax returns with income:	File joint tax returns with income:	File married & separate tax return	You pay each month (in 2019)
$85,000 or less	$170,000 or less	$85,000 or less	Your Plan Premium
Above $85,000 up to $107,000	Above $170,000 up to $214,000	not applicable	$12.40 + Your plan premium
Above $107,000 up to $133,500	Above $214,000 up to $267,000	not applicable	$31.90 + Your plan premium
Above $135,500 up to $160,000	Above $267,000 up to $320,000	not applicable	$51.40 + Your plan premium
Above $160,000 and less than $500,000	Above $320,000 and less than $750,000	Above $85,000 and less than $415,000	$70.90 + Your plan premium
$500,000 or above	$750,000 and above	$415,000 and above	$77.40 + Your plan premium

Beneficiaries who file an individual tax return with income:	Beneficiaries who file a joint tax return with income:	File married & separate tax return:	Part B Premium in 2019
Less than or equal to $85,000	Less than or equal to $170,000	$85,000 or less	$135.50
Greater than $85,000 and less than or equal to $107,000	Greater than $170,000 and less than or equal to $214,000	N/A	$189.60
Greater than $107,000 and less than or equal to $133,500	Greater than $214,000 and less than or equal to $267,000	N/A	$270.90
Greater than $133,500 and less than or equal to $160,000	Greater than $267,000 and less than or equal to $320,000	N/A	$352.20
Greater than $160,000 and less than or equal to $500,000	Greater than $320,000 and less than or equal to $750,000	Greater than $85,000 and less than $415,000	$433.40
Equal to or greater than $500,000	Equal to or greater than $750,000	Equal to or greater than $415,000	$460.50

The 2019 IRMAA income brackets above determine how costly your Medicare Part B (above) & D premiums are based on your income in 2017 (there is always a two-year lag). The higher income levels have been reduced by about $100,000 from the 2017 IRMMA brackets – which means more people paid higher premiums than in 2016. And compare the bottom income rows above and below too!

MAGI Reported on 2015 Income Tax Return (for 2017)		MAGI Reported on 2016 Income Tax Return (for 2018)		2018 monthly Part B premium
File individual tax return	File joint tax return	File individual tax return	File joint tax return	
$107,001–$160,000	$214,001–$320,000	$107,001–$133,500	$214,001–$267,000	$267.90
$160,001–$214,000	$320,001–$428,000	$133,501–$160,000	$267,001–$320,000	$348.30
Above $214,000	Above $428,000	Above $160,000	Above $320,000	$428.60

Again, notice the added 5th row of income levels for 2019! The "word on the street" is that these income levels will continue to be pushed downward – trapping more and more folks into higher Medicare B and D premiums. It's my personal belief that this will be another way for the government to "put a band-aid" on Medicare funding shortfalls at the expense of higher income people.

In any case, that's another advantage of the Get Me to ZERO™ strategies – distributions from <u>the truly tax-free</u> sources of income described in this book are NOT included in the IRMAA calculations and will NOT cause your Medicare premiums to go higher since it's non-countable retirement income. That is very important.

No matter how old you are, using outside money to pay your conversion tax bill effectively lets you shift money from a taxable account into a never-taxed account and lets you keep more inside the ROTH to enjoy forever tax-free growth. But using your own IRA money to pay for the government's share doesn't necessarily make a conversion a bad deal. You've still made a valuable tax shift!

One more point should be made on ROTH conversions. There used to be a wonderful planning trick and favorite strategy called "Recharacterization". I won't describe it here because the new Trump tax laws eliminated it. They took that planning tool away.

Anyway, every year I walk through the many advantages of ROTH conversions as an important step in the Get Me to ZERO™ strategy with some 50 prospective clients. Each of one of them comes away with a clear and full understanding of the benefits and a desire to make the conversion tax move. Remember, the more the IRS gets in your retirement – the less you get to spend.

Again, the income taxes must be paid someday -- at tax rates/ rules that have yet to be determined -- but that many economists, academics and experts believe will have to be higher than today's.

But here's a sad fact. Out of those 50 people, only 14-18 of them will actually write and sign the check to pay the tax to the IRS and move those funds to the never-taxed zone. No matter how well folks seem to understand all the many ROTH benefits intellectually, paying the taxes on that account now, is an emotional hurdle many people just can't seem to overcome. That's unfortunate.

And don't forget, that you have until you file your taxes to come up with the cash to pay Uncle Sam. If you convert in January, you have until April of the following year to save up money. That's over a year before taxes are due. You could adjust your withholding at work or add a line item to your monthly budget to save for the tax.

WARNING: Taxes are complicated and so are the conversion rules. I am not a CPA or tax attorney. I do not purport to know all of the rules, nuances, exceptions or "gotchas". Please discuss with a qualified tax professional before making any conversions so you will know exactly how your individual situation will be taxed, etc.

Section 72(t)

Why is there a 10% early withdrawal penalty? It's to discourage the use of deferred qualified retirement funds (payroll-based and IRA) for purposes other than normal future retirement income. So, the tax law has long imposed the additional 10% tax on certain early withdrawals. There are some exceptions which can vary based on the type of retirement account, but only one exception can help you move your savings into the Get Me to ZERO™ tax-free zone.

A couple pages back I wrote that I would describe a workaround to avoid the 10% early withdrawal penalty if you take money out of your traditional IRA before age 59½ -- although it's typically used for retirement income when someone retires earlier than that age.

It is a little-known section of the IRS tax code, §72(t)(2)(A)(v), which can be real handy if you happen to fit the requirements. For short, financial planners call this planning strategy: Section 72(t).

However, this strategy will NOT let you convert an IRA to a ROTH IRA. Therefore, if you want to convert to a ROTH before you attain that age, to avoid the 10% penalty, you will have to pay the income taxes from money outside of an IRA – probably money from your checking, savings account or a brokerage account.

Remember, there is really no way of getting around paying the income tax. Tax-postponed accounts are simply delaying taxes to the future – not avoiding them. We just want the future... NOW!

Normally, any distribution (other than specifically-qualified distributions such as rollovers and some exceptions) before age 59½ would result in a 10% early withdrawal penalty and 72(t) can help avoid this from an IRA (but not a 401K or similar plans).

However, "if" you participate in your company's 401K plan (and similar payroll-based ERSIA plans) and leave your job at any time during or after the year you reach age 55, there will be no 10% penalty for any taking early distributions from the plan. Of course, the income tax would be due on any tax-postponed account.

It is important to note that these "age 55+" distributions (versus age 59½ distributions) qualify only when you take them from a company defined contribution plan such as a 401K, TSP, 403B, etc. -- not an IRA account. IRAs don't qualify for this exception.

To keep the age 55+ penalty-free exception, the funds must not be rolled over into an IRA before you start taking distributions. The funds must be in a 401K or similar acct. to avoid the 10% penalty.

This is an important distinction you need to completely under-stand before doing a rollover to an IRA from your 401K, since a mistake would completely take away this 10% penalty exception.

FYI: The Pension Protection Act of 2006 made one more change to the rules: The age limit for this provision was reduced to 50 for retiring police, firefighters, and medics. These people can take early distributions from their work-based plans penalty-free at that age or after should they leave their job (but again - not from their IRA).

Here is how Section 72(t) works if you want to move your savings into the tax-free zone, are under the age of 59½ and you want to pay your taxes with your IRA funds... and avoid being slapped with the 10% early distribution penalty. In taking 72(t) payments from your IRA, you are taking "substantially equal periodic payments". These substantially equal payments must be made for the latter of: 1) five years minimum or... 2) until you reach age 59½.

It's for a stream of payments from your IRA... and not just a one or two-year withdrawal deal (again a 5-year minimum commitment period). You can start taking 72(t) payments from your IRA at any age you'd like – but distributions from that IRA will last for 5 years or until you reach age 59½ - whichever is longer.

The 72(t)-payment plan only applies to the IRA or IRAs from which you calculated your initial payment. You may split your IRA into two IRAs before setting up your 72(t)-payment plan. In other words, you can use one IRA to calculate and take your 72(t) payments, while another IRA can remain out of the picture for any other future use.

The 72(t) payments must be substantially equal and may not be altered or stopped during the payment term unless you become disabled or die. Your 72(t) payments can be monthly or annual.

There are three methods that the IRS has approved for calculating your 72(t) payments. For your own good, do not deviate from these 3 calculation methods. Those methods are 1) the RMD (Required Minimum Distribution) method, 2) the fixed amortization method, and 3) the annuity factor method. All three methods are based on your current age and the account balance of the IRA(s) that you plan on taking pre-59½ penalty-free withdrawals from.

It would be very wise to consult with a tax advisor to calculate your 72(t) payments, so you stay out of trouble.

The first method will produce smaller payments than the latter two methods. The RMD 72(t) calculation method is based upon your IRA account balance at the end of the previous year, divided by the life expectancy factor from one of these three IRS tables: 1) Single Life Expectancy table, 2) Uniform Lifetime table, or 3) Joint Life and Last Survivor Expectancy table, using the age you have already attained (or will attain) for that tax year. This required annual withdrawal amount will be different each year.

The 72(t)-annual payment under the Fixed Amortization Method is calculated by using the balance of your IRA account and an amortization schedule over a specified number of years. The number of years for your calculation is equal to your life expectancy from one of the above tables using the age you have attained (or will attain) for that year.

In addition, you will specify a rate of interest that is not more than 120% of the applicable federal mid-term rate (AFR) published regularly by the IRS in an Internal Revenue Bulletin (IRB). Again – don't try this at home! Get a tax pro to help you.

Your annual payment using the Fixed Annuitization Method requires you to take the balance of your IRA account and an annuity factor, based on your age and the current AFR rate.

I know that was much more information than you really wanted, but I want to make sure that you get qualified tax help in making your 72(t) calculations. You want the number to be correct and exact to avoid the 10% early withdrawal penalty.

Be aware, that if you do not stick to your 72(t)-payment plan, or if you modify payments in any way, they will no longer qualify for the exemption from the 10% penalty.

Not only that, but the 10% penalty will be reinstated retroactively to all the 72(t) distributions you have already taken. That means you'll have to pay back the penalty (and perhaps interest). You do not want to mess this up. It's easy to do this right and avoid issues.

Do not take any extra withdrawal as that would be considered a change of the original payment schedule. Any change in the IRA account balance, other than by investment gains and losses or the planned 72(t) distributions, would be considered a modification and would result in the 10% penalty retroactively. So, you cannot add any money to that IRA (either through rollovers or contributions) or take more money out. It must be left alone.

For the purposes of the Get Me to ZERO™ strategy we'll usually use the 2nd or 3rd payment calculation. Since we want to get the money out of the tax-postponed account as quickly as possible – keeping the tax-bracket management principle in mind too.

Again, 72(t) can only help you avoid the pre-59½ ten percent early withdrawal penalty. You cannot avoid the income taxes due. I have already written that the 72(t) cannot be used to convert to a ROTH IRA. So how do we get these funds into the tax-free zone? Where are the after-tax proceeds of 72(t) payments going to go? But first, let's understand a fundamental principle in tax planning.

Two Tax Systems in the United States

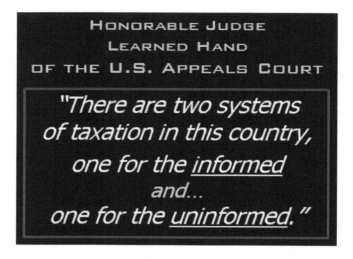

HONORABLE JUDGE
LEARNED HAND
OF THE U.S. APPEALS COURT

"There are two systems of taxation in this country, one for the <u>informed</u> and... one for the <u>uninformed</u>."

We have the absolute right to legally reduce our tax bill to the lowest amount allowed by Congress! This book aims to help you become one of the informed.

Judge Learned Hand (1872-1961) is perhaps the most famous U.S. Court of Appeals Judge to never became a Supreme Court judge. According to Wikipedia, he "was an American judge and judicial philosopher. He served on the United States District Court for the Southern District of New York and later the United States Court of Appeals for the Second Circuit. Hand has been quoted more often by legal scholars and by the Supreme Court of the United States than any other lower-court judge".

He also said, "Anyone may arrange his affairs so that his taxes shall be as low as possible; he is not bound to choose that pattern which best pays the treasury. There is not even a patriotic duty to increase one's taxes. Over and over again, the Courts have said that there is nothing sinister in so arranging affairs as to keep taxes as low as possible. Everyone does it, rich and poor alike and all do right, for nobody owes any public duty to pay more than the law demands". Well said Judge Hand!

That in a nutshell, is the legal basis for the Get Me to ZERO™ strategy – proactively and systematically arranging your financial affairs so that your future income taxes will be as low as possible.

This book is not about tax loopholes. Author Tom Wheelwright, CPA says, "After all, the tax law is really a map - a treasure map. As you follow this map, your taxes go down". If we can't eliminate future income taxes in retirement, we at least want to minimize them by becoming fully informed and proactively using the tax code as it is written and intended. Using our tax laws for future legal tax avoidance... NOT illegal tax evasion -- is being tax savvy.

Tax evasion (not reporting income) is how they put Mobster Al Capone in jail – not for his murders and other serious crimes.

Most tax preparers and financial advisors are focused on saving taxes now – not in future years. I guess that may make some sense in that many Americans are focused on instant gratification.

But let me ask you, although we know what inflation, health care costs and tax brackets/rates are today, are you willing to bet on what they'll be 20-50 years from now? You would only be making a tax rate mistake... if taxes go <u>down!</u> I'm not willing to make that bet. And that doesn't change all of the other issues and inflexibility with having so much of your savings in tax-postponed accounts.

My old boss, Pat Hegarty told me long ago, that it's often better to choose the devil you know... than to gamble on a devil you don't know. The devil I don't know, is future tax rates, rules and brackets.

Unlike Al Capone, I'm cheerfully going to pay my taxes "one-time" today – at rules I understand and at tax rates that I can easily live with (since I think taxes are "on sale" right now). I'm going to focus on what my taxes are likely going to be during my retirement (hopefully a retirement that lasts decades for at least one of either my wife and I – and my kids thereafter!).

I'm going to focus on what 100% of my account balances will be when I need them in retirement (and don't have to share with the IRS), rather than having account statements that do not show how much is the IRS's share of that money in the form of a future "tax lien". Your traditional IRA, 401K, TSP, 403B and other tax-postponed account statements tell you how much money is in the account --- but not how much of it is yours after paying taxes.

Which person do you think pays lower taxes, the informed person... or uninformed person? The proactive individual... or the submissive one? You know that smart people pay less taxes because they understand the system or use an advisor that does. And now you can too – by using as many financial tools as you can.

You want to look long-term and at the big picture when you build your tax strategy. Having too much money in tax-postponed accounts is short-term thinking. In return for a temporary tax reduction, you are trading flexibility, loss of access and control. You are also entirely subject to the IRS's future rules and regulations.

One final note on taxes. The discussion in this book is mostly about federal income taxes due to the IRS. But let's be clear, your tax bills don't stop there. Depending on where you choose to live, you will have other taxes and fees to pay (amounts will vary by location). Here is a partial list of your after-tax income supporting various government entities both today and during retirement.

There are state and local income taxes, real estate taxes, sales taxes, personal property taxes, car registrations, excise taxes (for gasoline, alcohol, cigarettes, sodas, hotel stays, airlines and many other items), tolls, licenses (driving, hunting, fishing, marriage, bikes, pets and so on) and special fees for courts, construction permits and dozens and dozens more. We are taxed and taxed!

We can't do much about these except choose where we live. But states that have no income taxes, usually have higher property and sales taxes. We really can't get away from paying most of these fees and taxes. But we can try and control our federal, state and local income taxes. So, let's keep on trying to do that.

TRIPLE ZERO™ Plans -- Strategy #3

Financial planning is a simple and focused process to meet a stated financial need or desire. It's not a product sale. Financial products/services are only "tools" that professional planners use to satisfy or meet a client's specific goal, objective or aspiration.

For many people, ROTH conversions and contributions will be all they need to do the heavy lifting for the Get Me to ZERO™ strategy.

ROTH conversions have much more potential "firepower" (no conversion nor income limits) than ROTH contributions due to the small $6,000 and $7,000 annual contribution and income limits. Renowned IRA expert Ed Slott, CPA tells us that "Uncle Sam is your partner in traditional IRAs and 401Ks, etc. So how do you get rid of him? The same way you'd get rid of any partner... you'd buy him out" (pay the taxes now). That's the ROTH conversion or the 72(t).

Paying taxes now is the "price of admission" to the tax-free zone. That way you can "look poor" on your retirement 1040 tax forms.

But there are millions of folks like me that either can't participate in ROTHs -- or need a powerful additional weapon in our arsenal to not only bring our retirement income taxes as close to ZERO as possible... but to have enough money in our tax-free accounts to enjoy 30+ years of a truly extraordinary retirement lifestyle.

As discussed in the section about 72(t), for those folks who are under age 59½ and want to shift money from their traditional IRA to the tax-free zone – USING the IRA money itself to pay the taxes due (and avoid paying the 10% early withdrawal penalty), the 72(t) rules can allow you to do that.

But as previously stated, 72(t) money is not a ROTH conversion. So where can you put this money to be in the never-taxed bucket? Tax Advantaged Life insurance (TALIC) is really the only other place.

The TRIPLE ZERO™ strategy is that additional powerful weapon to get to or close to our destination -- the tax-free retirement zone. As previously written, proper distributions from anything with the name ROTH in it... and life insurance will not show up on your future 1040 income tax forms. There aren't even lines to fill in for income from these (and other) truly tax-free sources on the 1040.

So you "look poor" on paper since so much of your cash-flow to enjoy your retirement years doesn't isn't even reported and of course, no taxes are due. Wouldn't it be great to receive $50,000, $100,000 or much more every year and legally not have to pay a dime of income taxes to the IRS or to your state? As an "informed" American, you get to keep 100% of those tax-free distributions.

Some financial advisors refer to the TRIPLE ZERO™ strategy as a private retirement plan. I call it a Tax-Advantaged Life Insurance Contract (TALIC). Now all cash-value life insurance policies might work, but most life insurance policies are not truly designed to be a ROTH supplement. Most would make an awful ROTH-alternative. As stated in the first pages of this book, the TRIPLE ZERO™ strategy is my Trademarked name for a special type of life insurance product.

Let's be clear, in my professional opinion, not just any life insurance policy will work well for this specific use. You need a type of policy (contract) specifically designed for this purpose.

Term insurance is an affordable way to protect your family from your early death. Most folks don't have near enough of it! With no cash-value, term life insurance won't work at all for this purpose!

What about whole life insurance? I don't believe that most whole life insurance policies are well-suited for this. They do have important guarantees (and you pay dearly for them) but they lack the necessary growth "horsepower" to really do a great job. There are a few whole-life policies that would be OK, but they would likely only provide about 40%-60% of the potential lifetime tax-free income of the TRIPLE ZERO™ policies that are best-suited for this purpose. That's a lot less future cash-flow for your premium dollars.

A traditional Universal Life (UL) policy generally has lower internal costs than whole life policies and market-driven interest rates but again, lacks the necessary historical growth potential to provide an increasing income stream for 20-35 years of retirement.

Although Variable Universal Life (VUL) policies do have the growth and accumulation "potential" needed (with multiple mutual fund-like investment choices called "sub-accounts"), they are also subject to huge market losses just like mutual funds. Like 401Ks, 403Bs and brokerage accounts, VUL policies can have big gains... as well as big losses (remember 2002 and 2008?).

Not only that, but the income distribution methods in VULs, ULs and whole life policies are not truly designed to provide maximum tax-free cash-flow. You need both growth and accumulation potential (without stock market risk) and an attractive and efficient way to take supplemental income distributions during retirement.

Each type of life insurance policy is built differently – although in all cases, the tax-free death benefit is the central focus and feature. The tax-free death benefit of all life insurance policies are very important and its true value should never be under-estimated.

How do you contribute to a life insurance contract? Well, you can contribute your after-tax dollars just like you would with a ROTH IRA. However, there are no annual contributions limits (like the $6,000 or $7,000 ROTH limits). Nor are there any IRS income limits that would prevent anyone from putting huge sums of money into a life policy. Your income can be as high as you can imagine, and you will still be able to fund your life policy. That's what I do.

If you are under age 59½, you can take advantage of the 72(t) rules (avoiding the 10% early withdrawal penalty) and shift money from a traditional IRA (pay your income taxes now) and fund your life insurance contract with the rest. That way you are converting money from a tax-postponed account into the never-taxed zone (assuming you follow the IRS rules). Yup, that's how we use a 72(t).

Cash-value life insurance has been used as a tax-advantaged accumulation vehicle for decades by numerous major corporations, small business owners, the wealthy and the "informed".

About 3,800 banks own $140 billion of bank-owned life insurance including ten major US banks that have over $60 BILLION dollars of their Federal Reserve "Tier 1 capital reserves" requirements safely invested in this SAME "asset class". If it's good enough for the Federal Reserve, shouldn't it be worthy of your consideration?

It's no gimmick or a passing fad. Now it can be your turn to take advantage of it. This fully IRS compliant "cash value" insurance planning tool is a near-perfect family protection, savings and supplemental retirement planning vehicle that was modified by three Congressional Acts in the 1980's (TAMRA, DEFRA and TEFRA).

So, let's take a closer look at TRIPLE ZERO™ - one of the best tax-free alternative retirement savings vehicle that Wall Street doesn't want you to know about. It's a prudent retirement strategy that offers "peace of mind" and a tremendous number of other valuable current "living" benefits that you don't have to die... to enjoy!

TRIPLE ZERO™ life policies have these three characteristics plus much more: 1) ZERO income taxation 2) ZERO stock market risk and 3) ZERO contribution or income limits.

I've already written about how proper withdrawals (following the IRS rules) from a life insurance policy are not subject to income taxes. We'll discuss this further on.

I've also written about how unlike a ROTH IRA and ROTH 401k (and similar work-based retirement savings plans), there are no contribution limits. One could fund a life policy with $100,000's a year. And unlike ROTH IRAs, life insurance does not come with IRS income limits – Congress not choosing who can and can't own one!

We'll talk about ZERO market risk and how that works in a moment but first off, what do I mean by a TRIPLE ZERO™ life policy. TRIPLE ZERO™ is my own name to describe a certain type of life insurance policy. A planning tool that has so many advantages over 401Ks, 403Bs, TSPs, traditional IRAs and brokerage accounts?

It's a specific type of a "tax-advantaged life insurance contract" (TALIC) called: Indexed Universal Life. One that can be specially-designed and maximum-funded for the Get Me to ZERO™ goal.

Index Universal Life, also known as an IUL, has many "living" advantages over traditional tax-postponed accounts that make it a perfect complement or perhaps an alternative to any ROTH.

Just like any IRA, 403B or 401K, your money grows tax-deferred. But like a ROTH, when you take money out of your account properly -- even at any time before age 59½ too -- you can access your money without any income taxes or 10% early penalties.

That's right, even accessing your earnings can be done tax-free according to tax laws on the books since 1913. And finally, just like the ROTH, when you pass away, your spouse or heirs get all of the money income tax-free as well. But the death benefit is much larger than the account. That sounds pretty good, doesn't it?

You get stock market-linked returns with NO downside risk to your principal (or even your past gains) due to stock market drops. No matter how much the stock market plummets, your worst annual return credited to your account is ZERO.

You completely avoid all market losses. Now that's a pretty safe, predictable and some would say: "stress-free" plan. Plus, you get the flexibility and security that allows you to comfortably stay invested in the market – even through all the economic recessions and bear markets you will likely face over the next 30-60+ years.

What if you knew that you would never have another losing year again and even your past gains would always be "protected" from future market losses? Do you think that you could stay invested in an asset that historically gave you 70%-85% of the market's returns, which over time beats inflation... and yet still sleep well at night?

According to Forbes Magazine on April 27, 2017: "Many people do not view life insurance as an essential and vital part of a retirement income plan. They see life insurance primarily as a way to protect families from the early loss of a breadwinner during the working years. However, life insurance has the potential to be so much more if properly utilized in a comprehensive retirement income plan." In fact, they can offer a lifetime of access, control and flexibility. It's become an important "asset class" of its own.

In that same Forbes article, "Russ DeLibero, CFP®, ChFC®, CLU® who also holds a Ph.D. in Financial and Retirement Planning, notes "that there are tremendous uses of life insurance in a retirement income plan because of the preferential tax treatment that life insurance receives. Both before and during retirement".

According to Dr. DeLibero, "When properly structured, life insurance can provide tax-deferred growth, tax-free cash flow, and a tax-free death benefit. The tax-preferential treatment provided to life insurance allows an individual to have greater flexibility over which dollars to use (before or) during retirement, and depending on the type of life insurance, it can also provide a non-correlated asset to the portfolio providing additional diversification." That's right, life insurance is a separate, non-correlated asset class.

Steve Jobs (co-founder of Apple) repeated this statement often, "People do not know what they want... until you show it to them."

The point of this book is to let as many folks as possible know what other financial tools and strategies are available to help them meet their retirement goals and dreams while enhancing their life today (while they are saving to retire). This book discusses seven of them. It's completely up to the reader to decide which, if any of these strategies might make sense for themselves.

Again, you don't have to even like life insurance. You just must like it more than you do paying future income taxes. Here's a quote from the Huffington Post website in 2013. All of the bullet points below will be fully discussed later in the pages that follow.

"Life insurance is a very powerful yet fairly basic financial planning tool that has been used to solve myriads of financial planning goals for decades. Some of the many uses of a properly structured and funded life policy include (words in parenthesis are mine):

• Creating a self-completing retirement plan (the tax-free death benefit to protect your loved ones from your early death).
• Providing supplemental retirement income for corporate executives, everyday employees (and the self-employed).
• Avoiding the threat of higher income taxes in the future." The Real Fiscal Cliff". (remember David Walker?).
• Addressing estate tax issues at death and paying off debts.
• Guaranteeing what you want to happen financially in life will happen, whether or not you are here (alive) to see it happen.
• Becoming your own bank and making more efficient purchasing (financing) decisions.
• Providing (nearly unfettered) access to funds that may be earmarked for retirement purposes (unlike IRAs, 40Ks, etc.)
• Having multiple investments uses on the same investment dollar.
• Paying for a college education without being disqualified from financial aid (unlike 529 plans).
• Addressing long-term care (LTC) needs later in life.
• Creating a (truly) tax-free income stream at retirement."

So, don't get hung up on the words "life insurance" – or you will really miss out! Nearly two BILLION dollars of cash went into newly purchased IUL policies from people just like you in 2017 alone. And the word is really just starting to get out about these powerful "private supplemental tax-free retirement" plans.

How TRIPLE ZERO™ Plans Work

Let's talk about this powerful financial tool which offers a death benefit, the safety of principal, ample liquidity, very good potential returns plus ROTH-like tax benefits and more. And even more importantly, there are no IRS contribution or income limits.

First of all, when we are using an IUL to accumulate cash, we do the EXACT OPPOSITE of what you'd do if you were buying life insurance only for the death benefit. So instead of looking for the largest death benefit for the smallest premium, we buy the LEAST initial amount of life insurance the IRS allows, and stuff as much cash into that policy as quickly as the IRS code 7702 will allow. That's the important key for the policy to accumulate tax-free cash.

Now there are various forms and slight differences between how the various IUL policies from different insurers work, but most work in the following or a similar way. The interest credited to your policy is "TIED" to a stock index – usually the S&P 500, over a 12-month period. Sometimes other market indexes and/or time periods are used in addition to the basic formula, depending upon the IUL policy you choose.

The S&P 500 index comprises the 500 largest public companies in the USA – Coke, AT&T, Apple, 3M, Boeing, Home Depot, IBM, Nike, Disney, Exxon, Walmart, Visa, McDonald's, Google, UPS, Proctor & Gamble, Starbucks, Microsoft, Goldman Sachs, Intel, Pfizer, GE, etc.

Now let's be clear, even though the interest credited to your contract is TIED to how well the S&P 500 index performs (excluding dividends), your money is NEVER actually invested in the stock market, which is why you cannot ever lose money due to market downturns.

My overall financial planning process always revolves around being fully defensive and prepared for the bad times - yet ready and opportunistic to profit in the good times. Each investment should have a defined "job description". An IUL does both very well and fully fits the bill for tax-free retirement planning.

Let me give a general description of how IUL's work and avoid stock market risk. As the name "Indexed" Universal Life implies, the interest "return" is determined by an index or indexes such like the S&P 500, Dow, Russell 2000 or the Barclays Bond index.

Many insurance carriers are even coming out with their own proprietary "blended" indexes to offer you more choices and more consistent returns in all types of economic markets. This is the latest innovation in TRIPLE ZERO™ plans.

Anyway, once you pay your premium (monthly, quarterly or annually) to the insurance company, the company invests those funds into their general account which is heavily invested in investment-grade bonds that pay interest.

The insurer could pay you an interest rate like a CD from what it earns on its own bond investments minus their overhead, expenses and profit margin. They call that their "fixed account". Your bank does something very similar, in that it pays the depositor an interest rate that depends on its loan portfolio interest income minus its overheard, expenses and profit margin.

As I write this section many IULs will offer their policyholders a fixed one-year rate of 3.5% - 4.5% or so (fixed account) right now. Way better than most banks, but not very appealing to most folks.

As the owner of an IUL, you have the right to forego getting that fixed interest rate and have those interest payments buy options on an index(es) such as the S&P 500, NASDAQ, Russell 2000, etc.

By using options, you can participate in the upside of the index when it goes up. But there is a catch – you usually don't get all or even most of the upside in a very good year. Because of the option strategy(s) you choose, you are "limited" in the amount of interest that can be credited to your IUL by a "cap", "spread" or a certain "participation" rate. I'll explain these terms in a moment.

Also by using options instead of investing your actual principal, you can never get a loss since your funds were never invested in the index. And the worst thing that can happen with the option strategies the insurer uses, is that the options expire worthless. When that happens, no interest is credited to your policy that year. In other words, you get a ZERO return.

When the stock indexes crashed as they did in 2000, 2001, 2002 and 2008, ZERO is your hero! It's much better to get NO return... then to experience a big loss. Your principal and past gains can never go backward due to market losses in an index.

And when the index goes up, because of the use of options, your gain is limited by either a cap, spread or a participation rate. A "cap" is the most the interest will credit one year (say 11%-13%), based on the index used, the cost of the options and the amount the insurance company can spend on the options (which is about equal to the interest they would have paid you in the fixed account). Historically, most indexes in IULs have used caps.

So with a cap, if the S&P 500 index prices gained 22% as it did in 2017, and your IUL had a 12.5% cap, that's the amount of interest that your IUL would have been credited with that year. Should the index earn 9%, since that is lower than the cap of 12.5%, you would earn the full 9% that year. Caps are best when the actual index returns are relatively low (under 8%) or just under the cap.

A "participation rate" means that you would get a certain percentage of the index's gain such as 60% -- with no cap on what you might earn that year. A participation rate can give you the potential for more upside in a BIG gaining year.

So with a participation rate of 60% and if the index went up by 30% like in 2013, your policy would be credited with an interest rate of 18% that year. When the index does 10% with a 60% participation rate, your interest credit would be 6%. If the index returned 4%, you would be credited with 2.4% that year. Again, you never participate in any index losses, so ZERO is always your hero.

Like participation rates, a "spread" also allows for some big potential gains when the index has large gains – with no cap! By "spread" the insurer uses that spread percentage to buy more options. A 4% spread means that you don't get any interest credited unless the index beats that amount (the spread).

But you get ALL of the gains above the spread amount credited to your policy. For example, if the index repeats 2013 and gains 30% with a 4% spread, your account would be credited with 26% interest. If the index returned 9% then you would get credited 5%. If the index only did 2%, the 4% spread is larger than the gain and you would get no (ZERO) interest that year.

Whether your index uses a cap, participation rate or a spread, in years like 2008 where there was a huge drop (-37%) in the S&P 500 index, many of my IUL clients proudly told me that "ZERO was their HERO"! Their IUL was their best performing asset since most everything else that they owned (stocks, mutual funds, real estate, etc.) went down in value and took years to "get back to even".

It's obvious that a ZERO percent return was awesome compared to a -37% loss. The main thing to know is that your account value can never decrease because the stock market goes down. You avoid all market losses. Your 401K can't do that for you. Even money invested in a ROTH, if it's invested in the directly in the stock market, it will decline in value.

Again, with a "cap", in years where the S&P 500 does well, your contract will be credited with an interest rate that is limited to a cap — say between 11%-13% a year. So, if the actual raw S&P 500 index goes up by 20% (excluding dividends), the interest credited to your account is limited by your policy's cap, perhaps 13%.

But whether your IUL uses a cap, participation rate or spread, (or all of them) unlike the actual S&P 500 index, your annual gains are always locked in and can never be lost by future market drops - ever. I'll write about "lock and reset" in a moment. This is huge and is one reason the TRIPLE ZERO™ plan is so stress-free.

Yes, those annual gains become principal and are never subject to market risk nor can be lost when the market goes down again... which it always has done. Some people may see caps as a negative, but if you never have to make-up for bear market losses and your past gains are protected forever, it's really tough to beat these products long-term performance of over 6.5%-9% gross average annual gains when you consider the valuable downside protection.

In fact, a policy with a 0% floor and a 13% CAP would have beat the raw S&P 500 index that had NO caps on its gains, nor limits on its annual losses, in quite a few single "15 year rolling investment periods" from the depression years through 2017 – with a lot lower risk and much less stress.

How does "indexing" work? The insurance company uses only the interest they earn from your premiums (they do NOT use any part of your premium/principal) to buy call options on the S&P 500 index (or whatever the index(es) being used is). If the index goes down, the options simply expire worthless and you get no return that year. But then the advantage of "reset" comes in. Wait for a few pages to learn more about this valuable feature.

So, you avoid all stock market losses. Neither you nor the insurance company losses anything except the fixed account interest your principal would have otherwise earned if the call options were not bought with that interest.

However, if the index goes up, the call options make a profit, and your account is credited with the full gain on the call options (up to the cap, participation rate or over the spread).

Neither you nor the insurance company can earn any more profit on the call options. Your principal never has market risk and you enjoy the potential to earn double-digit gains each year when the index does well. The worst thing that can happen is getting a ZERO % return in a bad year. You never go backward due to the market.

Your absolute worst years are 0% and your best are up to 11%-28% (averaging about 6.5% - 8% per year over time). When you combine the insurance company using only the interest they earn from your principal to buy principal risk-free options with the annual "reset" (described below), you get attractive potential account growth without market risk.

"Hope" is not a retirement plan – it's just another four-letter word. It's certainly not a plan that you can rely on. A properly designed IUL from a great insurer (AM Best "A" rated or better) along with ROTHs and other Get Me to ZERO™ strategies can provide the basis for a great retirement. Pay the IRS less and win.

Would you sleep better at night knowing your account can never lose money when the market goes down and yet you can enjoy (and keep) up to double-digit gains in years when the market goes up? Would never having a negative year again and protecting all of your past account gains be a good bet for you? Well, with no market risk one must expect to give up some market upside. There is no perfect place to save. But here's another advantage of the IUL.

The Powerful "Lock and Reset" Mechanism

Another important advantage to understand about TRIPLE ZERO™ plans is the "reset" mechanism. The power of the annual reset mechanism is that you get to actually grow your account when the market REBOUNDS after big stock market drops, while mutual fund and stock investors are hoping, waiting and praying just to get back to breakeven - back to before the crash happened.

Is your portfolio ready for the next market drop or economic recession? Will you be profiting during the eventual market rebound like IUL owners always do? The graphic below is an example comparing the IUL to a low-cost S&P 500 index mutual fund (excluding fees, expenses and dividends in both cases).

In the next hypothetical chart, the IUL and S&P 500 index are shown. Both have a $200,000 starting value. Let's see the Lock and Reset works and how they compare in "equity market rebounds" after a market loss. Let's say you had $200,000 each in your IUL and the S&P 500 index mutual fund on May 14th when the S&P 500 index was at 2500.

The first year the price of the index gained +12% (to 2800) so both products got that same dollar gain (since the IUL cap was 12%). Both accounts rose to $224,000 that year (excluding fees).

By May of the 2nd year, the index went down by -20% to 2240. As you'll see, if your IUL policy credited the "floor" of 0%, your contract account would still be worth $224,000 even though the market crashed. Your past gain was locked-in. ZERO was your hero.

Meanwhile, your S&P 500 index mutual fund would have gone down 20% in value along with the index with an ending value of $179,200. That's a loss of over $44,000 in the mutual fund.

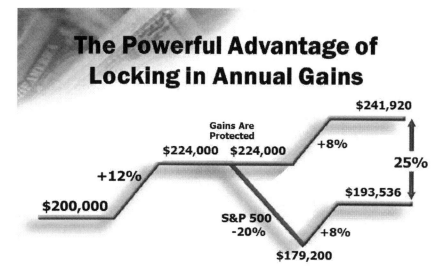

The Powerful Advantage of Locking in Annual Gains

$48,384 positive difference due to the annual lock-in and reset

In the IUL, we calculate the potential gain from where the index ended on May 14th of the year before (2240). During the next year, the index rose +8% to 2419. The gain of the first year was locked in and the $224,000 became principal in the IUL. But the mutual fund still must grow back to $224,000 before it gets back to break-even.

In the mutual fund, a +8% gain (from the index value of 2240 to 2419) on $179,200 value brings that account up to $193,536 at year-end. That's still over $48,000 lower than the IUL.

Even though the index gain for the IUL is calculated from the same 2240, the 8% index gain adds 8% to the value of the IUL. An 8% gain on $224,000 equals $241,920. That's a 25% larger value than the mutual fund. Of course, the mutual fund does not have a cap (participation rate/spread) slowing its growth in many years like it does in the IUL... but mutual funds can have big losses too.

And those losses in the fund must be made up for... before higher account values can be enjoyed. The $193,536 mutual fund will have to grow 40% to catch up to the IUL (assuming the IUL is capped out at 12% the 4th year – growing to $270,950 (not shown on graph).

That's a very important factor to consider. Losses must be made up for while the IUL keeps moving forward (although subject to a cap, participation rate or spread) and before all policy expenses.

Here's an analogy of a 0% floor and a 12% cap. Would you play blackjack if when you lost a hand, the worst thing the dealer did was to give you back your full bet without a loss? And when you beat the dealer's hand, you'd win up to 12% of your bet. And that 12% gain would be protected and could never be lost in future hands. If you knew that your chips were never at risk, would you keep playing? Most people would play that game all day long.

Of course, you can get the same protection from loss of principal if you invest in CDs and fixed annuities... but you generally do not get the potential of earning 11%-13% -- nor are those gains tax-free (unless they are invested in your ROTH).

You don't need to hit home runs to enjoy a great retirement. Just singles and doubles without any losing years will do the trick – especially with no future income taxes on your gains.

Warren Buffet said, "Unless you can watch your stocks decline by 50% without becoming panic-stricken, you should not be in the stock market". Do you remember how you felt in 2008?

If you want to take market risk, that's what the ROTHs are for (although these investments can be principal protected or have a good bit of risk mitigated depending on where you invest these funds – described in later chapters). The ROTHs give you tax-free income and if you want more market risk, I'd take it in your ROTHs.

The IUL gives you the same tax-free benefits, reasonable rates of return (but not the highest returns in a long, huge bull market) with protection from market losses. That's the risk/reward ratio.

So let's compare investing in the raw S&P 500 index to a hypothetical IUL policy. If you had $500,000 invested in the S&P 500 index on January 1st, 2000, and you took the actual historical annual returns of that index, including dividends but no fees, your account would only be worth $535,000 on 12/31/2011.

That's just a 1.07%% average gain on your money over those 12 years. Little actual growth but you'd have "real" losses for over a decade in "inflation-adjusted" terms. Your money would buy less. And you likely had a great deal of stress too with 4 negative years.

Could that happen again? Another lousy decade in the market?

However, if you were a 45-year old healthy male that put the same half million dollars into an IUL contract on January 1st, 2000, with a death benefit of $3.49 million dollars, your account value... the actual cash value in your contract would have grown to about $657,000 by the end of 2011 -- EVEN AFTER deducting all of the policy loads, insurance costs, fees and other charges.

Despite having capped returns when the stock market did very well, the IUL simply avoided the four years of market losses.

That's a difference of over $122,000 actual dollars in favor of the IUL in a decade of lousy stock market returns. And that insurance contract had a ZERO percent floor and a 12% cap. The S&P index went up by +16% (including dividends) in 2012? Would you rather get the full +16% gain on only $535,000... or get a 12% capped gain on $657,000? Which ending account figure will be larger?

Plus, the future performance of the stock market can never take those new gains away, since they would be locked-in and protected from the next recession and/or bear market. That's powerful and helps reduce your retirement worries. Don't you want to consider hedging at least some of your retirement risk and tax bets? Should you at least explore owning a small IUL?

And remember that if he died during that period, his spouse would get $3,469,000 income tax-free compared to the value of his S&P 500 mutual fund. You do get something for those policy fees!

I call that an "explosion clause". TRIPLE ZERO™ plans are "self-completing". In other words, if you die prematurely, the 100% tax-free death benefit instantly achieves your future savings goal.

So, your beneficiary doesn't have to worry about how they are going to save for retirement, the money will be there.

The statistics say that you'll probably live well into your 80's, but what if you die way before your time? The "what if"... is another big tax-free benefit of the TRIPLE ZERO™ plan just in case.

Now to be sure, I picked a bad 12 years in the market. So, let's take a broader look at the recent 28-year period: 1990 to 2017. We'll compare the S&P 500 Total return (including all dividends) to both an IUL with a 13% cap (excluding dividends) and one using a 4% spread (no returns until the index - excluding dividends beats the 4 percent spread). The "Annual Return %" column is the Total Return S&P 500 index and the "Limited Return %" is the IUL.

The chart on the left is using the 13% caps and the one on the right is showing the IUL with a 4% spread (with no cap). In both charts, the S&P 500 index (including dividends) but no fees had an average rate of return of +9.81% over the 28 years. That assumes the investor never panicked or sold during the 3-year bear market of 2000-2002 nor in 2008! I'd say that would be pretty unlikely and the well-known DALBAR investor studies seem to bear that out.

The capped IUL had an average rate of return of +7.59% over that time period. It captured 77% of the index's average annual gain without market risk or any stress during recessions and bear markets. It had more consistent returns than the spread and will perform better than a spread in a "not-so-great" market.

The IUL with the 4% spread had an average rate of return of +9.06% -- capturing 92% of the index's gain. It had years with much larger percentage gains when the index did great than the capped IUL... but it had a few more lower earning years due to the spread.

S&P 500 vs. IUL with 13% Cap

Year	Annual Return %	Limited Return %
1990	-3.10%	0.00%
1991	30.47%	13.00%
1992	7.62%	4.46%
1993	10.08%	7.06%
1994	1.32%	0.00%
1995	37.58%	13.00%
1996	22.96%	13.00%
1997	33.36%	13.00%
1998	28.58%	13.00%
1999	21.04%	13.00%
2000	-9.10%	0.00%
2001	-11.89%	0.00%
2002	-22.10%	0.00%
2003	28.69%	13.00%
2004	10.88%	8.99%
2005	4.91%	3.00%
2006	15.79%	13.00%
2007	5.49%	3.53%
2008	-37.00%	0.00%
2009	26.46%	13.00%
2010	15.06%	12.78%
2011	2.11%	0.00%
2012	16.00%	13.00%
2013	32.39%	13.00%
2014	13.69%	11.39%
2015	1.38%	0.00%
2016	11.96%	9.54%
2017	21.83%	13.00%

S&P 500 vs. IUL (4% Spread)

Year	Annual Return %	Limited Return %
1990	-3.10%	0.00%
1991	30.47%	22.30%
1992	7.62%	0.46%
1993	10.08%	3.06%
1994	1.32%	0.00%
1995	37.58%	30.11%
1996	22.96%	16.26%
1997	33.36%	27.01%
1998	28.58%	22.69%
1999	21.04%	15.51%
2000	-9.10%	0.00%
2001	-11.89%	0.00%
2002	-22.10%	0.00%
2003	28.69%	22.38%
2004	10.88%	4.99%
2005	4.91%	0.00%
2006	15.79%	9.62%
2007	5.49%	0.00%
2008	-37.00%	0.00%
2009	26.46%	19.45%
2010	15.06%	8.78%
2011	2.11%	0.00%
2012	16.00%	9.41%
2013	32.39%	25.60%
2014	13.69%	7.39%
2015	1.38%	0.00%
2016	11.96%	5.54%
2017	21.83%	15.42%

Most IULs use cap strategies and a few use participation rates or spreads. Picking an IUL based only on having the highest cap, lowest spread etc. is important, but it is not the smartest thing to do. There are some other very important components and features to making an IUL a great policy. I'll discuss those later.

Again, the IUL is a perfect supplement and/or alternative to your ROTH contributions/conversions. Of the seven Get Me to Zero™ strategies, these are the three most powerful. Although ROTHs have contribution and/or income limits, not everyone qualifies to get an IUL either. You, your spouse or someone else that you have a legal "insurable interest" in needs to be healthy enough to qualify for life insurance. There's a quick para-medical exam to complete too.

The whole aim of the Get Me to ZERO™ strategy is to make as much of your retirement cash-flow "invisible" to the IRS using the full tax code. Nothing different than Judge Learned Hand suggested so often. And the more sources of invisible cash-flow – the better!

Traditional tax-postponed IRAs, 401Ks, etc. are simply "tax wrappers". And the same thing with anything with the name ROTH in it. They are both tax-wrappers – not investments. They just describe how that investment is going to be taxed at distribution and perhaps some other rules like deductibility and RMDs, etc.

Both traditional IRAs and ROTHs can be invested in just about anything – CDs at your bank, stocks, bonds, mutual funds, annuities, etc. (although neither a traditional IRA nor ROTH can be invested in a life insurance policy). So besides explaining the tax and other ramifications of IRAs and ROTHs, I don't need to explain what a CD or a mutual fund is here. But that's not true for life insurance -- whether it's a whole life policy, variable UL or an IUL.

Most readers don't know much about or have pre-conceived myths about life insurance, hence so much detailed explanation about the

IUL and its potential part of your Get Me to ZERO™ planning.

Hopefully, you've learned a little about how interest in your IUL is credited to the policy – potential double-digit returns when the market does well and no losses due to bear markets and recessions. So, in addition to adding another potential source of tax-free income to your plan, you can also avoid stock market risk in the IUL too.

The financial planning software that I use in my personal practice is Circle of Wealth®. The founder and CEO of that company is a very smart man named Don Blanton. He has come up with a pretty concise explanation of life insurance called the 10-minute lesson (a snapshot of it below). I'll take less time than that here.

Why would anybody pay $20,000 annually for a $500,000 death benefit when their sex, age and health would allow them to buy the same amount of death benefit for just $1,000? Obviously, the buyer must be getting a lot more than just a death benefit.

You've probably already guessed that the $1,000 premium is for a term insurance policy. Maybe one that fixes the premium for 10-30 years. Who determines and sets the price (premium) for that term life policy? The insurance company does. Not you and not the IRS.

And what does the policyholder get with a term policy? Usually only a death benefit should he/she die during the term. It's like renting versus buying a home. It's less expensive because relatively few people actually die while their term life insurance is in force.

Am I suggesting that buying term insurance is a mistake? Heck no! Most people don't have nearly enough death benefit protection and "term" is a wonderful way to affordably protect your loved ones. But a term policy will not give you any cash-flow in retirement.

Now, who do you think sets the $20,000 maximum premium for the same death benefit in a permanent life insurance policy (PLI) for the same person in this example? The insurance companies? No. It's the government who sets the maximum. Yup, it's the IRS who determines the max premium amount one can put in that $500,000 policy in this example (based on the sex, age & health of the insured).

In the 1980s TAMRA (Technical and Miscellaneous Revenue Act) and DEFRA sets the minimum death benefit according to a complicated formula that allows for a policy's favorable tax treatment. They boil down to what's called the MEC limits (Modified Endowment Contract) which would make withdrawals from your policy... taxable. Nothing wrong with a MEC policy in and of itself, but we want to avoid a MEC policy in the Get Me to ZERO™ strategy.

Whether the policy is a MEC or a non-MEC, the death benefit is always tax-free (except in some pretty rare situations).

Of course, if you'd like to put more than $20,000 premium in (for the Get Me to ZERO™ strategy) you'd just have to buy more death benefit. So there really is no practical annual premium limit to get you the supplemental tax-free income you're looking for.

The MEC limits don't determine the amount of premium you can pour into a policy, just the minimum amount of death benefit that amount of premium must purchase (depending upon your sex, age and health). MEC limits also apply to how fast you can put money into your policy. To avoid a MEC in an IUL (a quick rule a thumb), you generally can't fund it any quicker than 3 years and a day (if you're under age 50) and 4 years and a day if you're older than that.

For example, my buddy out in Denver has a wealthy client putting $500,000 a year into his minimum death benefit policy. I can't recall if he's paying that premium for 4 or 5 years and then they will stop making premiums payments. There are 1,000's of people putting in at least $1 million a year into life policies. Some, $10 million/yr. or more.

Without really getting in the technical weeds on this, the big difference between a non-MEC policy and a MEC policy is how they are funded and how any distributions out of the policy will be treated for taxation. With the MEC, any earnings taken out of the policy will be taxable and a 10% penalty would also apply if the owner was under age 59½ - (sounds like a non-deductible IRA to me). So, for Get Me to ZERO™ planning – we definitely want to avoid a MEC.

Now if the government is regulating the most premium you can put into the policy – what does that say about it? It says that it must be good – and "good" for you in relation to your income taxes. The premium limits for tax-free retirement cash-flow fall right below the MEC line. Don Blanton calls the MEC line – a "Maximum Efficient Contract". The difference between taxable… and tax-free.

A non-MEC policy is a Tax-Advantaged Life Insurance Contract (TALIC). That's what you want for another source of non-taxable cash-flow in retirement. By "maximum funding" your policy with the "minimum death benefit" – it brings you right below the MEC line.

On the right side of the chart above, you can see a list of many desirable benefits one would like in a savings vehicle. A non-MEC policy can provide them all – except for the one listed at the bottom – "Deductible Contributions". You don't get that one. Darn! Oh well.

The more you contribute to your non-MEC policy, the greater the degree of those listed benefits you'll enjoy. By funding your policy with less money, you get fewer benefits. Also, by fully funding your contract, you reduce the internal costs of the policy (as a percentage of your cash value) over your lifetime and increase your net returns.

With the wealth-building goal of TRIPLE ZERO™, you want to focus less on the size of the death benefit (which the MEC line will determine for you) and more on the amounts you feel comfortable contributing to this portion of your Get Me to ZERO™ plan.

Depending upon your sex, age and health you can contribute a similar amount to a ROTH ($500 a month) up to $100,000 or much more a year. You can fund your TRIPLE ZERO™ policy for 20-30 years or longer -- or complete paying for it in just four or five years (and anything in between). The policy funding design can be very flexible.

Now your stockbroker, advisor or know-it-all neighbor will say that cash-value life insurance policies have expensive loads and fees and charges and that is very true... ESPECIALLY IF it is NOT structured properly to accumulate and grow your cash with the minimum death benefit allowed by the IRS rules.

Your policy needs to be properly designed by someone who really knows what they are doing and who is only looking out for your best interests.

Over your lifetime, IUL policy expenses will ONLY cost you about .8% or less a year. That's about what many equity mutual funds charge you to chronically "underperform" the stock market. Historically, a fully-funded IUL contract should have an actual cash-on-cash, TAX-FREE internal rate of return (IRR) of between 6%-7.5% over the long-term -- even after ALL insurance loads, fees and charges are deducted. I'll show some client examples in a few moments. All without market risk.

You would need to consistently earn a pre-tax rate of about 8%-12% a year to equal that tax-free rate of return -- depending upon your personal IRS and state and local income tax bracket.

And since we are all going to pass away someday, at least the tax-free death benefit gives you something of VALUE for your .8% or so of long-term average annual policy expenses. Most actively managed "buy and hold" mutual funds can't honestly say they add any value over indexing, but they still charge you each and every quarter of every single year. They get paid in the awful years... or the good ones.

If you've watched the YouTube video about high 401K fees -- (many 401K plans can cost you 1.5%-3.5% each year) which can actually "rob" you of $100,000's in total lost retirement income. That's in addition to taking on all stock market risks, having virtually no access to your money, causing your Social Security to be taxed as well paying those postponed taxes on your future income at unknown rates/brackets.

Now if you are thinking about putting money in an IUL (or any cash-value life insurance policy) and taking most every penny out of it within 5-8 years (basically surrendering the contract), then this isn't the right financial vehicle for you. Don't do it. These policies are built for the long run as you'll see in a moment. Remember the tortoise and the hare. Steady wins the retirement cash-flow and tax race.

But if you want steady long-term performance, safety and complete flexibility (plus good tax-free cash-flow down the road), a properly designed and funded IUL is a great supplement and/or alternative to the ROTH. Don't forget that economic recessions happen about every seven years, and with an IUL's lock and reset, you'll never have to recover from another one again. Combined with any ROTH strategy, the TRIPLE ZERO™ plan can add tremendous lifetime value for you.

No other financial vehicle can match the benefits of no market risk, double-digit potential returns when the market does well, the annual reset, access to your cash pre-59½ and tax-free distributions. And the death benefit is a huge "bonus" for your loved ones if you happen to die too young. But the real benefit is for YOU... if you <u>live</u> a long life!

Some client examples....

Tim is one of my Texas clients and he's a 47-year-old male who is worried about future increases in income tax rates and the potential of reduced Social Security benefits for all but the poor. Right now, he can only comfortably afford to contribute $600 a month to his IUL in addition to the $5500 annual ROTH contribution and he plans on doing so (but is in no way committed to do so) for 19 years - until age 66.

The minimum non-MEC death benefit for his age and health is just under $150,000. A 30-year term policy would cost him a bit less than $50 a month. But Tim was looking "invisible" retirement cash-flow to supplement his ROTH – not a death benefit. He already has a $1 million 20-year term policy to protect his wife (plus coverage at work).

If Tim makes all the planned contributions and we average just 7% gross annual rates of return (not the historical crediting rate of 8.3% as it did over the last 25 years in this policy, so I'm being conservative), he could start drawing $16,000 per year of TAX-FREE income from his policy at age 67... for the rest of his life. I think it will likely be more.

And keep in mind that we all have a rising income problem (due to inflation). So, his initial income of $16,000 could increase by 3% each year. When Tim is age 80, it could be $22,800 a year and at age 90 it could be $30,600 a year and keep increasing by 3%. If Tim passed away at age 93, he could have enjoyed over $575,000 of tax-free distributions from his IUL – after ALL policy fees, costs and expenses.

Again, that's after ALL insurance policy costs, expenses and fees (which are mostly front-loaded in the first 10-15 years). Now that may not sound like a lot of income, but remember it took him a whole 19 years to contribute a total of only $137,000 into the policy. If Tim put in the same amount faster, his results would have been even better.

At age 93, his cumulative net internal rate of return (IRR) on his 19 years of paid premiums was 7.3% (after all fees and expenses). And that 7.3% IRR was after-tax since this cash-flow does not show up on any tax returns (just like cash-flow from a ROTH). So, depending upon future tax rates, it can be equivalent to an 8.5% - 12% pre-tax return.

And since this is life insurance, his spouse or kids will eventually get a net death benefit of over $250,000 tax-free (at age 93) on top of those policy distributions. The total of "living" and death benefit from his $137,000 contributions could be up to $825,000 TAX-FREE or more.

During the early years, his policy expenses are high, but they don't stay high forever. At age 75 for example, he still has about $247,000 of cash value left in his policy and the total of policy expenses for that year is $516. That is a total policy cost of just .002% during that year. After decades, the IUL expenses have become much less of an issue. TRIPLE ZERO™ is a long-term income program – not a 100-yard dash.

All of his income projections above are based on an average of +7% gross interest credited to his policy from the various index methods that are available to him in this particular policy. As I mentioned, the historical returns over the last 25 years were +8.3%, so I am being conservative in my forward projections for his gross interest-earned.

I have another 52-year-old client in Georgia who transferred about $94,000 from an older life policy (via a 1035 tax-free exchange) and is planning to make 13 years of $75,000 annual contributions into his newest IUL for a total of $1,069,000. This is his 4th IUL policy with me.

He earns too much money to contribute to a ROTH and does not have a ROTH 401K at work. Like me, the IUL is his best tax-free alternative.

I'll call him Dan. His initial death benefit is over $1.3 million and like the gentleman described above, it will increase with each premium payment for maximum growth of his cash-value. Unless you are just going to make premium payments into your IUL for 4-5 years, having an increasing death benefit helps maximize your cash accumulation.

Anyway, using the same 7% projected average annual returns (when the historical returns have been over +8.3%), at age 67, the cash value (after about $186,000 of up-front policy expenses and fees have been deducted over that full time period) should be over $1,500,000. That's a lot of expenses and they do bring down his tax-free internal rate of return (IRR) to just 4.44% during those first fourteen years.

But in the 15th year, his policy expenses are just $2,766 that year. That's a total expense of only .0019% that year. Less than 2/10ths of a percent of his $1.5 million cash-value. Cheaper than Vanguard!

At age 67 Dan should enjoy $100,000+ a year in tax-free cash-flow from this TRIPLE ZERO™ policy alone. At that point, Dan's death benefit will have grown to about $1.8 million. So, either Dan himself or someone that he cares about is going to be well taken care of.

Although it's his largest IUL, he will have "invisible" distributions (legally not shown to the IRS on the 1040 tax form) from his other three IULs too. Remember that Dan doesn't qualify for a ROTH. And none of this huge cash-flow will make his Social Security taxable!

That $100,000 annual income should grow by 3% a year to mitigate inflation for the rest of his life (doubling to about $200,000 a year by age 90). At that age, Dan's cumulative IRR will have grown to +6.88%. By age 90, he'll already have received over $3.4 million in tax-free cash-flow from this TRIPLE ZERO™ policy. Should he pass away that year, the net death benefit to his loved ones and/or charity will be $1.4 million. Although if Dan is still alive beyond age 90, the growing tax-free distributions will still be paid every year. Not a bad alternative to a ROTH, is it? Pay the IRS less. Keep more and have a better life.

The IRS contribution limits won't allow you to contribute $75,000 a year into a ROTH 401K – even if one was available to him at work. So how else is Dan going to save enough for the retirement lifestyle that he envisions and avoid annoying annual 1099s from a taxable account.

I truly believe that his income will actually be greater than what I projected (and his IRRs too). Even a +.25% increase in his projected +7% average returns will make a big difference since all the policy expenses have already been fully deducted. And there is another reason that the income will likely be higher in all my client examples shared here – it's called "loan arbitrage" and I'll fully explain that later.

In any case, there's nowhere else to put that amount of money that will be tax-advantaged for the rest of his life. Not only that, but he has unfettered access to his cash surrender value at any time (we'll discuss the "private reserve" strategy in a later chapter too), no market risk, lock and reset and a giant death benefit should he get hit by a bus.

Jennifer is a 36-year-old Florida client who is contributing enough money to get the full match into her company ROTH 401K. Then she decided to add to her retirement savings by putting away $1,000 per month into an IUL until age 66. The lowest initial death benefit in her case (per IRS tax regulations) starts out at $497,000. It will grow to over $1.6 million dollars by the time she retires at age 66 from her total of $360,000 in contributions ($12,000 x 30 years) and using +7% projected average returns (lower than historical crediting rates).

Like all life insurance, her beneficiary would get a huge death benefit if something awful happened to her – but we "built" this policy for "living" benefits for Jennifer and her family. She can access some of the cash in her policy anytime and for any reason (estimated to be over $460,000 at age 56) – without any taxes or penalties - even before retirement. A powerful part of the Get Me to ZERO™ strategy!

At her retirement age of 67, she could start taking planned tax-free distributions from her policy of $77,000/year (growing at 3% a year for the rest of her life – even if she lives to age 120). This income will not cause her Social Security to be taxed nor show-up on her tax return.

And Jennifer's had no stock market risk nor any market stress along the journey. But let's say she gets hit by lighting at age 86. Over just those 20 years she would have received over $2 million dollars in tax-free withdrawals from her IUL and she would still leave a tax-free net death benefit of $1.3 million dollars to her loved ones.

And if she didn't pass away at that age, her tax-free annual income would have grown to $135,000 a year (and continue to grow by 3% annually for the rest of her life) and she would still leave a substantial death benefit behind. After-tax money "in" – all tax-free money "out".

Here's a teaching moment. I usually like to spend-down ROTH and IUL money "last" during retirement (each person's situation and goals are different though). In Jennifer's written retirement income road map plan, I have her delaying taking any money from the IUL for just 5 more years. Everything else being equal, that could increase her initial tax-free annual income from her IUL to begin at $110,000 (instead of $77,000) and still growing by 3% annually thereafter.

That's a $33,000 bigger income to start with (plus larger annual increases). Nearly 50% larger income and potentially $100,000's more total tax-free lifetime cash-flow by delaying just five years!

To review once more. Why is having supplemental non-taxable income in retirement important? According to an article in the April 1, 2018 edition of Fortune magazine, the federal debt has tripled from 2007 and it will probably double again by 2028. "To ensure long-term (fiscal) stability, policymakers (Congress) will have to do something that's been almost unthinkable in recent memory – simultaneously cut spending and pump up revenue" (taxes). Parentheses are mine.

That's what David Walker has been saying to anyone who will listen since 2010. Getting as much retirement cash-flow off the IRS's radar screen as possible, is simply smart tax-diversification. Anyway...

Now I wrote earlier about people under age 59½ that want to convert their traditional IRA to a ROTH, but don't have the funds outside of the IRA to pay the income taxes due. And for these folks, the 72(t) can provide the answer to use some of the IRA money itself to pay the IRS the taxes due (don't forget tax bracket management).

You'll recall that 72(t) cannot be used to fund a ROTH conversion. So, if you want to get more of your savings into the tax-free zone (the Get Me to ZERO™ strategy), the only other truly tax-free place to put those funds, is into a well-designed and maximum-funded (TALIC) life insurance policy. Do you still hate life insurance? Or hate taxes more?

Again, under the tax laws, any permanent life policy will work. But in my opinion, the structure and benefits of a great IUL contract make it the superior choice. A distant second choice would be one of a couple select whole life policies – but you'll sacrifice future income.

Steve is a married 46-year-old man with $430,000 sitting in an old 401K from his previous employer that he wanted to rollover into an IRA (step 1). He fully understood the benefits of a ROTH conversion, but did not want to pay the tax out of his taxable brokerage account. Nor did he want to pay the 10% early withdrawal penalty by using his own IRA money to pay the federal and state income taxes.

He had about $360,000 in a brokerage account and he is getting nervous about being in the tenth year of a bull market. He's moved $45,000 of his account to a money market fund for any emergencies.

Steve spoke with his CPA about taking advantage of some capital gains in the account – selling some stocks at their highs. Again, he wants to keep tax bracket management in mind, but not let the "tax tail... wag the dog". It's better to pay taxes than take a big loss sometimes.

Anyway, he wants to move some $15,000 a year from his brokerage account (net of capital gains taxes) into the TRIPLE ZERO™ plan too.

Finally, his new job does offer a ROTH 401K and he is going to max out ($19,000 for under age 50) his contribution and get the company match, rather than just contribute the $12,000 to get the full $6,000 match. Like millions of American, his income is too high for him to be allowed to contribute to a regular ROTH IRA.

So calculating his 72(t) amount (based on his age, IRA balance and the current applicable interest rate), he must take $19,807 out of his IRA, pay the income taxes due (avoiding the 10% penalty) until at least age 59½. However, he plans to continue moving the tax-postponed IRA into the IUL until he retires at age 66 (21 years).

After paying taxes of 28% (22% federal and 6% state), he'll have $14,261 available to pay the IUL premium plus the $15,000 from his brokerage account for a total of $29,261 per year into the IUL.

With the insurance carrier we chose, the minimum initial death benefit was $596,192. His wife Teresa liked the fact that she had some valuable additional financial protection, should the worst happen to Steve. They still have 3 kids at home. The death benefit would increase each year while Steve was funding the policy.

Using a conservative +7% average annual gross return from the multiple indexing strategies within the policy, when he is finished funding his IUL, it should have some $1.2 million of net cash value and the death benefit will have risen to about $1,876,000 – after all policy loads, fees and expenses had been deducted.

Along the way, Steve will have the opportunity to take advantage of $100,000's of his policy's cash-value by using the Private Reserve strategy to potentially profit by having his savings working in two places at once (upcoming chapter). You can't do this with any ROTH.

When Steve retires at age 67, he should be able to enjoy $86,000 of annual tax-free cash-flow (growing at 3% each year) until age 120. This would be in addition to tax-free income from his ROTH 401K. None of this income would cause his Social Security income to be taxed either.

It's unlikely that he'll live beyond age 100, so let's say he passes away at age 92. That year his annual invisible IUL income (unseen by the IRS and state) will have grown to $174,000 or so and he will have taken a cumulative $3.1 million out of his IUL policy and Teresa would still be left with a tax-free death benefit of $1,360,000 at that point.

Jason is a 62-year-old man who just inherited some money from his mother. After paying some bills, making two ROTH contributions and planning a very special 30-year anniversary trip to Europe, he wants to put $150,000 into a TRIPLE ZERO™ plan. He wants to position this money in a place where, unlike a taxable brokerage account, he won't get annual 1099's for interest, dividends or capital gains.

He does not want any more stock market risk than he is already taking in his traditional 401K. He also worries about owning bonds in a rising interest rate environment since he understands that rising interest rates generally causes the value of bonds to go down. And most "fixed" bond income has a hard time keeping up with inflation.

He has had a few health issues in the last 8 years, but he's in pretty good health now. Although his doctor says he should lose 20 or 25 lbs.

As I wrote earlier for someone about age 50 or older that wants to fund his IUL as quickly as possible and still avoid a MEC contract (to keep the tax-free advantages), he can fund the policy at $30,000 a year for five years. Then his contributions to his policy are complete.

Since this is a short-pay situation (4-7 years of contributions), it's usually more efficient for accumulation to have a level death benefit (rather than increasing). In Jason's case, it's just under $359,000.

Due to his older age and potentially a shorter time until he may want to take some money out of his TRIPLE ZERO™ IUL, I used a more conservative 6.5% gross average annual interest crediting rate from a selection of indexes available to him in this policy. Again, I think he'll get closer to +7.5% over time. Perhaps even close to 8%.

After all policy fees and expenses, at age 75, Jason would have just under $197,000 in cash-value inside of his policy. Just for kicks, I ran a quote for him on a 15-year term policy for $150,000 death benefit (the difference in year-13 cash value and his actual $359,000 death benefit). The best quote from an "A+" rated carrier was $1,590/ year.

So nearly $20,600 of the fees and expenses he's paid in his IUL policy so far went towards the insurance costs for the death benefit he would have paid for in that term policy. Now I understand that he really wasn't looking for a death benefit. He was more interested in a tax-advantaged place to put some of his inheritance, but the death benefit does have a real value (that he paid for) which reduced his gains over time. And the term insurance would have expired in two more years. He would have just "rented" a temporary death benefit.

Like Jennifer, the longer Jason leaves the money in the policy, the faster the cash value will continue to grow. That will start pushing up the cash value to about $500,000 at age 89 and nearly $1 million at age 100 (and the death benefit will grow as well).

Of course, since he avoided a MEC in order to get tax-free access to his cash at any time, whenever he needs some of that money, he won't have to worry about what tax rates, brackets or deductions might be at that point. Any cash distributions will not show up on the 1040 tax form. The same tax result as anything named "ROTH".

And IUL's aren't only for younger folks. Many seniors can truly benefit from them as well. It's also a great CD, money market, bond or annuity alternative too. Bill is a 70-year-old male in normal health with $250,000 sitting in low-interest and taxable CD's that he wasn't planning on ever touching. We moved that money into an IUL contract all at once (single premium), with an initial death benefit of $401,000.

As you may remember, putting too much into a life policy too soon will make it a MEC contract. Rather than a TRIPLE ZERO™ plan, it's only a "double-zero" plan. A MEC keeps the 1) unlimited contributions/no income limits and 2) no stock market risk (with the lock and reset) attributes – but does forfeit the tax-free nature of any distributions. However, his money will grow tax-deferred – no annual 1099 forms reported to the IRS if he doesn't take any money out of his policy.

Illustrating an annual average crediting (earnings) of +7% -- EVEN AFTER deducting ALL of the insurance policy loads, fees and charges -- the accumulation value in Bill's contract would have safely grown from $250,000 to about $332,000 in just 10 years - all tax-deferred. There's little chance his CD's could do that nowadays. His cash safely grew by $82,000. His death benefit grew too - it's $443,000 at that point.

And if Bill died anytime during that period, his beneficiary would get at least $401,000 dollars income tax-free. In fact, his policy's cash value and death benefit will likely grow to about $587,000 and $681,000 respectively, over the first 20 years and keep increasing if he never touches the cash in the policy. Your CD money can work harder.

But... if Bill ever needs or wants to get some cash out of his policy to supplement his income (say at age 85), he could do that too. Under the same assumptions he could take $3,000 out of his policy every month until age 100. That's a total of $540,000 potential income for himself plus he would still leave a death benefit of $146,000 to his loved ones. Being a MEC however, the distributions would be taxable until he was withdrawing his basis (the $250,000 premium paid).

All of those benefits came from a $250,000 single premium -- moving money from a low-interest, taxable, sleepy, boring CD to a no stock-market risk alternative. It's a great alternative for "LAZY MONEY" – but one needs to be healthy enough to qualify for life insurance. If Bill's health didn't qualify, then perhaps his wife's health would have. Or perhaps even one of his children.

Let's look at the opposite end of the age spectrum – Bill's first grandchild - a one-year-old grandson named Jacob. Unlike a ROTH, where one needs to have "earned income" to qualify to contribute to one, a 15-day old baby in normal health can qualify for a TRIPLE ZERO™ plan. There are a few caveats such as the parents must have life insurance on themselves and all children must be covered, etc.

I understand that baby's do not need life insurance, but what better place to get them financially started and positioned for the rest of their life. Let's see how this might play out for Jacob's future.

Bill wanted to fund Jacob's IUL at $200 a month for the next 25 years. That's a total inheritance to Jacob of $60,000 over that time. Bill will own the policy and control its cash value, naming any beneficiaries, etc. until he passes it to Jacob's ownership in the future.

For a male baby of that age, this policy had an increasing death benefit that began at $254,000. But death benefit was not the primary motivation for Bill. It was to start a savings account, free of all stock market risk that Jacob could access for any purpose, at any age – with no taxation (no pre-59½ issues that even a ROTH IRA would suffer).

Left untouched until age 31, there might be some $220,000 of cash value in the policy with a death benefit of over $607,000. That cash could be used to fund a down payment on his first home, a business idea or it could be simply left inside the policy. It's a perfect source of "private reserve" money that I'll write about later – allowing Jacob's savings in the IUL to do two jobs at once.

However, all that aside, should Jacob just leave the money in his TRIPLE ZERO™ plan until retirement at age 67, there should be some $4.3 million of cash value and the death benefit should have grown to about $5.1 million to protect his own future loved ones.

There are a number of ways to improve that policy's performance too. Jacob could decide to continue to pay the $200 monthly premiums at age 26 himself or anytime thereafter for example.

What a wonderful legacy Bill is leaving for Jacob. Why aren't more insurance agent's all-over this type of planning? Well, the 1st year commission is only about $600 for this policy. For most agents, that's not worth the hours of explaining the benefits of this concept to both Bill and Jacob's parents too... plus doing all the necessary paperwork.

While we're on the subject of children and IULs, let's take a moment and compare an IUL with a 529 plan college savings plan.

As a former practicing college-funding planner, I could write pages comparing a properly structured and funded IUL to a 529 plan, but let me just mention a few reasons why many of my savvy clients will decide on using an IUL instead. Firstly, a parent or student-owned 529 plan is a "countable asset" in all financial aid formulas.

But life insurance (and annuities too) and retirement accounts are specifically EXCLUDED assets on the FAFSA form and for all other college financial aid forms - except for about 3 dozen universities and colleges. A 529 plan can reduce your financial aid where any permanent life insurance policy will not. That could be a big deal.

Secondly, the IUL is a self-completing plan. By that, I mean that if the "breadwinner" passes away – the death benefit will immediately complete the college savings plan. But again, the IUL can be a superior "tool" if you live. And it does so by avoiding stock market risk along with the powerful lock and reset feature. They are valuable benefits.

Money in a 529 plan can only be accessed tax-free if it's spent on qualified educational expenses while an IUL can be accessed for any purpose on a tax-free basis – as long as you follow the simple IRS rules. Perhaps you'll need the cash for something before college, or your child gets a "full ride" or even decides not to go to college at all. Yes, there are some solutions, but none of them are perfect.

An IUL has much more flexibility. And unlike a 529 plan, an IUL can avoid stock market risk while offering double-digit gains in the good years, has the annual lock and reset to profit from stock market rebounds -- while the 529 plan is trying to make up for lost ground.

Ok, enough on 529 plans. They certainly have value, but like every other financial product they do have their shortfalls as well.

Anyway, I could go on and on with more examples of TRIPLE ZERO™ plans and how many folks fund them, but you probably have the idea by now. There are literally 10,000's of these types of plans bought every year to the tune of about $2 Billion dollars in brand new policies.

And as I previously wrote, 100% of my own retirement savings are my contributions to five TRIPLE ZERO™ policies. I can't do a ROTH and in any case, although not perfect, IULs give me almost everything I'm looking for in a place to store my money. Especially if you believe like I do, that taxes "must" go up at some point to pay for so many huge unfunded government promises… that are still being made to us all.

I'm sure by now, you have "googled" IULs and much of what you have read about them on the internet is very different from what you are reading in this book. At the end of my book, after going through the rest of the Get Me to ZERO™ strategy, I'll address and dispel each of those falsehoods and myths. Do you think I own five IULs to have made a commission from myself? No, I bought them for my lifetime benefit. Out of my own and my family's best interest. But only you can decide if an IUL would add value to your own retirement planning.

Ok, to continue explaining how IULs work, I'll discuss in detail, how you access your money from them. I'll then describe the Private Reserve strategy and how this feature alone can make a TRIPLE ZERO™ plan much more valuable for you and your family before retirement.

After that, I'll write about how some folks can actually use OPM (Other People's Money) to help you fund a huge TRIPLE ZERO™ plan as well as how some business owners/contractors (and millions of other folks) can do some cool things with funding them as well – using OPM (Other People's Money). We'll finish up our discussion on IULs with some miscellaneous information and things to ponder before getting to the 4th component in the Get Me to ZERO™ strategy.

Accessing Your Cash

Throughout the last number of pages, I've described a number of clients and how they've funded their IULs and the conservative projections they are looking for in terms of non-taxable supplemental cash-flow during their retirement. So how do they access their cash and why is it tax-free (assuming they follow the simple IRS rules).

There are basically three ways to get access to your cash surrender value in your TALIC (Tax-Advantaged Life Insurance Contract).

The first way is to take withdrawals of your basis (the amount you've paid in premiums so far). When your policy is designed to be a Maximum Efficient Contract (not a MEC), you can take out your basis from the cash surrender value at any time. Since the IRS sees this as "your own money" (after-tax premiums paid), it is not taxable income.

However, in a Modified Endowment Contract (MEC), any earnings or interest comes out first – which would be taxable... until you are down to just the basis in the contract (not taxable). As discussed, there is nothing wrong with a MEC in and of itself. But you definitely do not want to have your policy become a MEC for a Get Me to ZERO™ plan.

Nothing wrong with taking a "withdrawal" from your life insurance contract – but just understand that it is a withdrawal and not a loan. Any withdrawals from the policy can never be paid back and therefore cannot be available for future your use (Private Reserve strategy).

Just like with a ROTH, once you take a withdrawal you can never put that money back into the ROTH. It's gone from the never-taxed zone.

The second and third methods of accessing your cash in the policy are two different types of loans. They can be repaid (or not) back into the policy and would be available for you to use again and again. There are no credit checks. There are no coupon books to repay the loan. No amortization schedules. No required monthly payments at all.

As you know, when you get a loan to buy a car, a home or purchase something on your credit card – that loan is not taxable income. The bank doesn't tell the IRS that you borrowed $50,000 to buy an SUV and you don't pay income taxes on the bank's money because it's not income… it's a loan that needs to be repaid.

It's the same thing with taking a loan from your insurance contract. It's a loan, that if you do not repay it while you're alive, it will be repaid out of the death benefit. More on this in a moment.

One thing that gets me so mad, is when an uneducated insurance agent tells someone that they are borrowing their own money out of the policy and are just "paying themselves back". That is untrue. Sounds good, but they have no idea what they are talking about.

You are borrowing the money from the insurance company and the cash surrender value in your contract is the <u>collateral</u> for the loan. Since the insurance company has full collateral (and no stock market risk of declining like a "margin" account at your broker's), there are no credit checks, questions about what you want to use the funds for and no loan applications. It's a pretty simple and quick process.

The insurance company is delighted to loan you the money. They are fully protected and secure with the collateral. Your loan collateral and the interest receivable is more secure than a corporate bond.

Did you know that Walt Disney took a loan out on his insurance contract to help get his company going? More recently, so did Doris Christopher, the founder of Pampered Chef (now owned by Warren Buffett's Berkshire Hathaway). Collateral secured by the policy cash value. There's many more folks that have started a business or weathered hard times with the funds from inside their life contract.

Before I get started with this, let me say that each insurance company seems to have a different name for their loan option(s). This can be confusing, but they mostly work in one of the following two ways. Some insurers offer one loan option only, a few offer both.

The first type of policy loan is often referred to as a "wash loan". It is either a no "Net" cost loan or has a small guaranteed interest rate (usually 1% or less). The terms and interest percentages will vary by insurer, as well as how many years the policy has been in-force.

Here's how a typical "wash loan" might work. On any amounts loaned from the policy, the insurance company may charge you a guaranteed interest rate of 4% while at the same time crediting the loan balance with a guaranteed 3.5% interest earned. That would leave you a net interest cost on the loan balance of just 0.5%.

The interest rates charged and credited may be different and hopefully as low as a guaranteed 0% or .25% loan cost once the policy has been owned 6-10 years or so. In any case, it's pretty attractive.

It's important to note on this loan type, any outstanding loans are not participating in any index(es) growth. So loaned amount interest credits are calculated per the above, with no chance of growth in the index(es), while un-loaned funds can have full gains (caps, spreads).

The other type of loan doesn't sound as attractive at first, but over time, I think it is certainly so. Again, it goes by different names. I like the name "participating" best. I like the word "participating" because under this loan option your full account balances (including loans) can participate in the index growth (or a 0% return in a negative year).

How the insurance company charges interest under this method varies. Most insurers have their interest rate "floating" with an index like the Moody's Bond index or perhaps the Prime Rate. This can be an attractive option when interest rates have been very low such as over the last 5-8 years. But those interest rates can go sky high as well.

There have been many periods when the Moody's and similar bond indexes have had rates of 7%, 8%, 9% and even double-digits. I'm not very comfortable with being locked-in forever to a loan interest rate that I have no control over. Personally, I prefer the next type of loans.

A few other policies have a guaranteed participating loan rate of 5% to 6%. All loans will always be charged that specific guaranteed interest rate – no matter what the Moodys/Prime rates are (lower or higher). Some have a floating loan rate that will never be lower than say 4%... or never higher than 6%. Depending upon interest rates in general, there is a guaranteed range of loan costs that you know in advance. I like this certainty of knowing how my interest will be calculated and that it has a maximum interest rate. I can plan for it.

So why is a loan rate of 4% or 6% potentially more attractive than a "wash loan" (maybe <1%, although I've seen net rates as high as 4%)?

Well, I've already given you a hint. Under this loan regime, ALL of your cash value is able to participate in the index gains. If you believe that over time that the index will return about 7% or more on average and your loan cost is guaranteed to be under 6%, then you have an attractive loan arbitrage opportunity. Loan arbitrage is how your bank makes money. Pay low-interest rates on CDs, lend out at higher rates.

If you could borrow at a guaranteed 6%... and you could get an average 7% return, how much would you borrow? I'd borrow as much as I could. As long as I could be pretty confident that my policy would earn more than my 6% loan costs over time. When the index gets capped out at 12.5% and my loan cost is 6%, I've made a 6.5% arbitrage profit from the loan within the policy. I got paid a profit to take a loan. However, on the other side of the coin, if I get a 0% interest credit one year when the stock market tanked, I'd have a 6% interest rate loss that year. There's that risk/reward again.

Since 2015, the new NAIC rules only allow IUL illustrations to show a maximum of 1% loan arbitrage on loan balances. But I believe the reality will be about 1.5% over time – so the tax-free cash-flow should be higher than projected in my client examples a few pages ago. But again, I like to make conservative projections and plan to beat them.

The 15, 20 or 25-year crediting history of many of the indexes used in the IULs have historical average rates of returns that exceed +7.5%. Some are well over 8.25%. So, I feel pretty comfortable with projecting future income distributions using +7% average interest earnings over time – especially with a guaranteed maximum loan interest rate.

There are even a very few insurers that will let you switch from one type of loan (wash loan) to the "participating" loan as often as once a year. That gives you the best of both worlds. You can use the wash loan when you think the markets will go down (protection in the few bad years) and use the participating loan when markets are doing well (most years) to take advantage of the potential positive loan arbitrage.

As I'm writing this page, I just saw a commercial on CNBC talking about margin loan rates on a brokerage account like Schwab, Fidelity, etc. If you're not familiar with brokerage account margin loans, you can generally borrow up to 50% of your stock holdings at fluctuating rates. Those rates just mentioned on the commercial were over 7.5% and those interest rates are not locked in. They can go higher or lower.

But unlike a margin account at your broker, you will never get a margin call from your insurance company because of a market crash (or one of your stocks crashed like Enron) since market losses do not occur in the IUL like they can (and will) happen in the stock market.

You will get a brokerage margin call when the value of your loan balance is more than 50% of the value of your portfolio. So, if you borrowed $75,000 from your $150,000 brokerage account and the portfolio value drops to $140,000, you'll need to add another $10,000 right away or they'll start selling your positions from under you. There were lots of margin calls in early February 2018 when the market dipped about 10% within a few days from all-time highs.

I had a margin loan called back in 2002. They told me to deposit another $20,000 by the next day. I did and then I had to send another $6,000 the day after that. That was enough. I closed the account!

Anyway, of course any loan or withdrawal from a life policy will lower the net death benefit to your loved ones. That makes common sense. If you repay the loan, the death benefit gets restored as well.

And here's the most important thing to know and keep forever in your mind about IUL loans. You never want your policy to lapse for any reason, including taking too much money out of it. You MUST die with your life policy in force and a death benefit must be paid to your beneficiaries. They will get whatever is left over after paying back the loan (retirement cash-flow, etc.) and any outstanding interest due.

If your policy lapses before you do (death), all loans and interest will become taxable. The insurance company will send you a 1099 and believe me when I say, that you will not want to pay that tax bill. To prevent that from ever happening, most policies have an over-loan protection rider which would pay-off the loan and interest and reduce the death benefit down to $10,000 or something, so that you die with that death benefit in force and never get a taxable 1099 form.

Of the two loan types, the "wash loan" is the most conservative and will likely produce the lowest lifetime tax-free cash flow while the participating type-loan will offer the most potential for higher income. They both have their place and that's why I love the few IUL's that allow you to switch loan methods as often as every policy anniversary.

Again, many IULs do not allow you to switch loan-types at all... while others may only allow one loan switch during your lifetime. That's not optimal. All things being equal – loan flexibility is a huge advantage. Not only while taking lifetime tax-free monthly distributions during your retirement, but in conjunction with the next chapter as well.

Private Reserve Strategy

Now that you have a good understanding of how policy loans work in a TRIPLE ZERO™ plan. I'd like to explain the Private Reserve strategy that I've referenced many times already. In a nutshell, this strategy revolves around having your savings work for you in two places at once – by using 2nd type of arbitrage. It's the same way that banks money. Pay depositors a little interest, loan out their money for more.

When I wrote about the potential loan arbitrage above (earning 7% in the policy with a loan maximum of 6%) that was primarily about how you can increase your retirement cash-flow from policy loans from a TRIPLE ZERO™ plan. Since your accumulation value (the value invested in the various indexing options) is never going down because of loan distributions (although your loan balance increases each year), you can profit from the 1% positive loan arbitrage in this example.

But the private reserve strategy is used while we are accumulating the savings in your policy – not during the Get Me to ZERO™ income phase of the plan. It is meant to add to your total wealth along the way -- in a manner that is not possible with a ROTH 401K or ROTH IRA (or any retirement plan for that matter). It's a strategy that allows you to have your policy funds earning returns in two places at once.

First and foremost you need to understand that this strategy is only for serious savers and investors – not spenders. You want your money to grow in two places and not just grow in one (IUL) and be spent along the way... leaving you with a loan balance in your policy that will decrease (or perhaps even eliminate) your supplemental tax-free cash flow in retirement. Investing wisely... verses spending.

So as just mentioned, when you take a participating loan out of your IUL, it does not reduce your accumulation value earing interest (but a wash loan does). So, there is more upside with that type of loan, while there are times (when you anticipate a bear market that the wash loan is a great one to switch to if your IUL allows it).

You'll also recall that the loan comes from the insurance company's checkbook – with your cash surrender value being used for the collateral. That's why there's no loan applications, credit checks, explanations of why you want the money, etc. For simplicity sake here, let's assume that you own an IUL with a fixed (or at least a capped loan interest rate) of 6%. The highest guaranteed loan rate.

Collateral capacity is the amount of funds you have available in your life insurance plan to borrow against. The more you fund and the longer you own your IUL, the more collateral capacity you'll have. It's a valuable resource for you and your family. Treat it wisely.

The ability to access capital, no matter what the economy is doing, whether you are employed or not, without completing invasive and personal credit applications, credit checks and without questions about what you want the money for, is a wonderful feeling. And the ability to get capital within a week or two can make you wealthier.

In the private reserve strategy, you borrow most of your cash surrender value in the policy and <u>invest</u> it somewhere else that you believe will easily earn more than 6% (NET after paying taxes) since this loaned money is now outside of the "tax-free" TALIC zone.

I believe, your indexing strategies in the IUL with the 0% floor (no losses from the markets) along with the powerful combination of locking in and protecting all past gains from market losses (lock) and the "reset" mechanism... will give you something close to or better than an average of 7% gross interest crediting per year over time.

The indexes in the policy are going to earn, what they are going to earn. Probably more than 7%, but maybe less over a bad 10 or 15-year period. Borrowing money from inside the policy to invest in a second place will not affect your IUL – as long as you pay the insurer back.

The financial "hurdle" that you need to jump over in the private reserve strategy is how much, after paying income/capital gain taxes, will your second investment make you. In this example, the after-tax net earnings hurdle must be over 6% a year (or whatever the interest rate you are owing the insurance company) policy loan cost.

Remember that you'll want to pay the insurance company back with interest (put the loan amounts back into your IUL). And since you want to pay the insurance company back, your second investment should be very reliable. I would never invest in penny stocks, raw land, Bitcoin (or any digital currency), etc. with proceeds from a policy loan.

If you want to speculate on any of those or a long list of other high-risk investments, I would never recommend using a loan to do it. That's simply reckless in my opinion. This is your retirement money!

Could you pay off high-interest credit card debt with a 6% loan from your IUL? Sure, that may make sense if your credit card interest rate is 15% or more. That's a 9% positive arbitrage. However, what my experience as a financial planner has taught me, is that once many folks pay off their credit card loans with a HELOC, 401K or any other lower cost loan, these folks tend to run the credit cards right back up again and are now in a worse position. They owe money to the HELOC, credit union or insurer... and have brand new credit card debt to boot!

That's not a good thing. It's a good idea gone wrong! Would I use my policy to finance a car like so many agents are pushing now? Absolutely not. My current car loan is at 2.15%. I wouldn't use the collateral capacity inside my policies for something like that. It's much too valuable – even if I couldn't get a car loan for under 8%.

Personally, I won't take out a loan from any of my policies unless I'm pretty certain that I'll get an after-tax return of at least 10%-12% in 12 months or less. I don't want to speculate and take undue risks.

The following is NOT investment advice nor a recommendation. But I know many people (clients, my advisor friend's clients, etc.) that have used their collateral capacity to invest in real estate rehabs, real estate flipping, hard money loans and tax liens (all with the underlying property as collateral – an added layer of protection).

I've heard of using loans for invoice factoring. A car dealer who finances cars. One retired car salesman who buys cars at auctions (using policy loans) and sells them. I'm told that he has "flipped" as many as 6 cars in a month using one policy loan.

With the stock markets up so high now, I would never borrow from my policy to invest in stocks at these levels. But my thinking might change after the next crash. One of my close advisor friends bought either Procter and Gamble or McDonald's stock (I can't recall which) in 2009 with a policy loan and reaped some very good profits over the next 18-24 months. He thought the risk was worth the reward.

But he will not recommend to his own clients that they ever invest in the stock market with proceeds from a policy loan. Neither will I.

The point here is to be as wise as you can with your collateral capacity. Invest/flip/rehab in something you know about – especially if it has collateral (real estate, car, boats, etc.) with a short turnaround (no longer than 12-24 months). The shorter turnaround the better.

At the least, make sure that you'll get your loan amount back, so you'd just lose the interest paid to the insurance company. Cut your losses and move on to the next opportunity. Learn from any mistakes.

Meanwhile, you are enjoying uninterrupted compounding and growth in your TRIPLE ZERO™ policy. Your loaned money never left the policy and it continues to grow based on the performance of the index strategies you chose. The policy values are simply collateral.

Before I go on, I'll just make a quick comparison with a ROTH. I love ROTHs as you know, but like an IUL, they are not perfect and have shortcomings like everything else in this world. No IRA (ROTH or traditional) can be used for loan collateral. It's against the law. So, there is no way to do the private reserve strategy with a ROTH.

Once you take money from a ROTH, you can never put it back. It's gone from the tax-free zone forever. ROTH funds have no way of increasing your wealth in two places at once. It's either growing inside of your ROTH... or outside if you take it out – not both places.

One of original IUL mentor's clients had over $1 million dollars of cash value sitting in his IUL – which, as you'll see in a moment, is the absolute best "parking garage" for your money. At the height of the last financial crisis, he had a great opportunity to buy a foreclosure on Hilton Head beach. The condo was worth over $625,000 back in 2007.

If he could get the money within 10 business days, he could buy it for $478,000. He simply faxed the insurance company who quickly sent him the money (since it is fully collateralized with his cash value) so he could close on the condo and take advantage of this great deal.

It had a long history of earning nearly $43,000 in annual rental income – that's a 9% cash-on-cash annual return on the rent. That more than covers his 6% interest cost. And that doesn't include any potential appreciation as we eventually came out of the recession.

So he can simultaneously earn rental income from the condo (pay back the loan to the policy over time) and continue to get potential double-digit gains from his IUL policy as the stock market rebounds from last recession (past gains were locked in and the indexes reset).

He can then sell the condo in a few years at a big profit when the real estate market gets better or keep it by refinancing it with a traditional mortgage and pay back the full policy loan within a few years. Put the funds back into your financial "parking garage" and wait for the next profitable business opportunity to come along.

Like all policy loans, there are no structured loan repayments. No coupon books. No loan amortization schedules. He doesn't need to pay the policy loan back at all... or even any interest either. But not doing so would likely put his plans for invisible retirement cash-flow from his policy in peril. Always pay back your private reserve loans!

No other "lender" will give you more flexible repayment terms than your personal TRIPLE ZERO™ can. Paying back that loan and interest replaces your collateral capacity, giving you access to capital to take advantage of opportunity after opportunity. All the while your funds inside of the TRIPLE ZERO™ plan earn 0%-13%+ or so each year.

Using your IUL as a "parking garage for your cash" and as a private reserve account can really TURBO-charge your net-worth. It's a safe parking place that you don't have to wait until you retire... to use it. You can get profitable pre-retirement access, benefits and flexibility that you cannot get anywhere else (at least not on the same terms).

Here's another important financial point to learn, embrace and teach your children about major purchases. Many wealthy folks tell me they pay cash for everything (except perhaps their real estate). I guess there's nothing wrong with being debt-free. I certainly oppose having consumer debt to fund one's lifestyle. But they are forgetting an important financial truth about paying cash for everything.

Are you ready to learn it? You finance EVERY SINGLE BIG THING you buy! Because you either PAY interest to finance or lease those things... or you LOSE the interest and investment income that you could have earned if you'd kept your own money invested instead.

Now most folks think that they SAVE interest by paying cash for purchases and that is true. But that's only half of the story. The full truth is that "you either pay someone else interest to use their money or you lose the interest you would have earned by using your own cash instead". This is an economic law. A financial truth.

Unless the funds you use to pay for something were hidden under your mattress and not earning any interest, you are actually giving up all the interest/growth those savings would have earned by using your own money and not financing. Not only do you lose interest this year, but your lost interest is compounded year after year after year.

That's called lost "opportunity cost". Of course, your savings have to be earning higher interest than your interest cost to consider financing as described. But just know that you're always financing — one way or the other on any major purchase.

With the private reserve strategy, your funds inside of the policy (assuming you are using a "participating loan") continue uninterrupted compounding --- without having to give up an opportunity to take advantage of other select and carefully thought-out investment opportunities. Assuming just a 1%-1.5% private reserve arbitrage, you could possibly add up to $100,000's of more wealth over 20-30 years.

Let's change gears again and get back to the TRIPLE ZERO™ plans.

But I heard that "life insurance is a bad investment"! Well, life insurance is not an investment. It's life insurance with a death benefit and premium payments. However, based on what you've read so far, would you agree that it is a pretty good place to store and build your wealth that also offers very favorable tax-advantages? And with the IUL structure, is it a place to avoid stock market risk while having the potential for double-digit gains when the market does well?

From what you've read so far, if it wasn't called "life insurance" and there was no death benefit (that you do pay for) would this type of "parking place" for your money be pretty compelling as a long-term supplement to all your ROTH strategies?

The death benefit is what gives life insurance all of its many tax advantages. Tax advantages that have been part of cash value policies since 1913 when income taxes began in the U.S. And I've never known a life insurance agent to have been kicked out of a house when delivering a big death benefit check to a beneficiary. Not once.

How much life insurance would you want if it was free? All you could get? I would too. So, it's not life insurance that folks aren't excited about, it's paying for it – (usually for the benefit of somebody else at our death). With the TRIPLE ZERO™ strategy, we reduce those mortality costs to the lowest possible (assuming your policy is structured to be as efficient as possible) for our own "living benefits".

That's right, in addition to the death benefit component (especially in the early years), we try to maximize the benefits to you and your family while you're alive and well. That brings us to the next potential benefit of an IUL (and some other life insurance policies too).

Long-Term Care Benefits (LTC)

It seems that everybody who knows how much long-term care costs (in a home, assisted-living or nursing home), is concerned about if they and/or a family member will need care for an extended period of time someday. How will they handle that potential financial burden? It's probably the most feared but least prepared-for "risk" that too many Americans have. And that financial fear is well-placed and valid.

When I was 40, I bought my own traditional LTC policy. Smartest thing I ever did (assuming I don't die in my sleep). But today, these policies are much more expensive and harder to qualify for based on your health. And there is no getting around the "use it… or lose it" nature of traditional LTC insurance policies. Traditional LTC insurance sales today are a fraction of what they were in the late 1990's.

But that doesn't make the risk of you or your spouse needing LTC go away. The risk of needing care and its potential costs are still there.

There are many life insurance policies that offer an alternative to traditional LTC insurance policies. And some annuities do too. They require much bigger premiums, but at least there is a benefit to the family if you die never needing LTC care – the death benefit or annuity account value. I won't go into all the types of life insurance policies that also offer some sort of LTC benefit – over and above the actual death benefit in this Get Me to ZERO™ strategy book.

But what I will do as appropriate here, is briefly discuss general information as to the LTC benefit in some IUL policies. Some have no-cost LTC benefits… while others charge a cost for an LTC "rider".

There are basically two types of LTC benefits in many TRIPLE ZERO™ policies should you need assistance in 2 of the 6 Activities of Daily Living (eating, bathing, toileting, dressing, transferring and incontinence) for a period that's expected to last at least 90 days… or have some type of cognitive impairment such as Alzheimer's.

In one type of LTC benefit, the IUL insurer would advance you part of the death benefit in the amount of perhaps 2%, 3% or 4% a month in order to help pay for your care at home or in a facility.

However, since the IUL is a life insurance policy, it was priced on your likely death somewhere in your 80's. If you have a stroke at 68 and need care, they will be paying out part of your death benefit, about 15 years too early. So the IULs with no-cost LTC benefits will typically discount the death benefit (based on a formula) and pay that 2%-4% monthly advance of the reduced death benefit since they are paying it way earlier than your original life expectancy.

The IUL policies that offer a LTC rider for a charge (which reduces your policy cash accumulation) will not discount the death benefit when they advance you the funds to help pay for your care at home or in a licensed facility. In either case, every advance of your death benefit will reduce both your cash value and eventual death benefit.

If you are primarily interested in having LTC protection on your IUL policy (rather than income), I would consider paying for the rider (which is a cost drag on the accumulation value). However, here's why I wouldn't pay for an LTC rider on a TRIPLE ZERO™-designed plan.

By definition, the TRIPLE ZERO™ plan is designed to minimize the death benefit – particularly by the time you are taking tax-free cash-flow out of the policy. So, there won't be much difference in the amount of your death benefit and the cash surrender value in your policy. You'll likely be better off just keeping the tax-free distributions coming in. It was originally structured to supplement ROTH income and reduce your income tax burden to as close as ZERO as possible.

In the TRIPLE ZERO™, unless you have an LTC care "event" early in the policy, neither a paid LTC feature nor one included at no-charge is going to be that big of a benefit. But just like if you die early in the early years, having an LTC need with an LTC benefit in the early years can be of great value! But under normal circumstances, the LTC rider is not nearly as valuable as many insurance agents make it out to be.

Those agents that try to "sell" someone on the idea of having both LTC protection (when they are old and more likely to need it) and the tax-free cash-flow at the same time, either don't understand how the LTC benefit really works or... well, I'll just leave it at that. No comment.

Trade-in the Old for the New?

For some strange reason, life insurance is the only industry that tries to keep people from "trading in" their obsolete products for a newer, improved version. Maybe it's time for a policy upgrade.

You may have a whole life or some type of universal life insurance policy in force already. Even though you are older now, it sometimes makes absolute financial sense to do a tax-free exchange (1035X) from the old kinds of policies to a new one which has new benefits & lower mortality costs due to the fact that we are living longer than before.

If you already own a cash-value life insurance policy, it may (or may not) be to your advantage to consider doing a 1035 tax-free exchange of an old policy into a TRIPLE ZERO™ plan if it's your desire to Get Me to ZERO™ or even to just help financially protect against an LTC event. Basically, once you get health-approved by the new insurer, you can instruct them to request the funds in your old policy to be transferred directly to the new one which would cancel the old policy.

The CSO mortality tables are put together by the American Academy of Actuaries, which is an 18,500+ member professional association whose mission is to serve the public and the U.S. actuarial profession.

The internal insurance costs in all life insurance policies are largely determined by the CSO mortality table used. But over the years as our nation's longevity has increased, these mortality tables have changed – getting a lot less expensive (by 30% to 50% or more).

Since 2009, all life policies issued must use the 2001 CSO mortality tables. Any policy issued before 2001 (and perhaps through 2008) is burdened with old, outdated life expectancy mortality costs (1980 CSO mortality rates). If your policy was issued prior to 1980, those CSO mortality costs (set back in 1958) are another 30% more expensive. The new 2017 CSO tables are coming over the next few years too.

A new IUL can have less expensive internal mortality costs (using the newer CSO life expectancy tables) even though you are older now. The bottom line is that your current life policy (even an outdated IUL) is likely costing you too much. BUT more importantly, it may be leaving other "new and improved living benefits" off the table for you and your family. That's true even if your annual premiums are "paid up" or are being paid out of the policy cash values or from dividends.

Moving your old policy to a new TRIPLE ZERO™ one could improve your retirement cash-flow. Or you can possibly get a larger death benefit, stop ongoing premium payments… or get a new policy with enhanced Long-Term Care benefits at no out-of-pocket cost to you.

Plus, unlike an older Universal Life or Whole Life policy you get the chance to safely earn up to 11%-13% when the markets do well and benefit from the lock and reset. Why settle for a low fixed-rate return when you can have the chance to earn up to double-digits when the markets do well. Or take advantage of much better policy loan terms. For example, I just saw a 2008 (issued) IUL with a 4% guaranteed "wash loan" cost but it's at "only 2%" now. Yikes! Are you kidding me, a 4% guaranteed wash loan? We are doing a 1035 exchange today.

You just might need to have your old policy carefully analyzed to see what may be best for you today. Based on my experience, you'll likely be very pleased with the policy analysis and your options to make a substantial policy improvement – if you are healthy enough. Be certain that all of your existing life policies are pulling their own weight and that your family would not be better served with a brand new one with better interest earnings strategies, loan terms, etc.

FYI: If you would like, my team does in-depth life insurance policy "audits" every month, at no cost and without any obligation. Just let me know if you are interested. No medical exam is needed to do our initial due diligence report. Of course, never, ever cancel your current policy until the new one is fully in-force.

Catapult Your TRIPLE ZERO™

The next few pages of opportunities may not be available for just anyone to take advantage of, but they should be interesting at the very least. But that changed a bit 3-4 years ago for about 5 million Americans who might now qualify – and perhaps many readers of this book who become extremely interested in Get Me to ZERO™ planning.

Financing life insurance premiums has been around for decades. However, it has been (and continues to be) mostly for the wealthy – those with a net worth of at least $8 to $10 million dollars (excluding their primary residence). It's OPM (Other People's Money) in action.

Why use your own funds (which hopefully are earning much more than the cost to borrow) to pay for life insurance. It's called Premium Financing or Premium Funding – and its big business for some life insurers. Most "big dollar" premium finance programs (there are a few great ones and several ones I would not recommend to my worst enemy – so buyer beware!) – are used for estate planning, buy/sell agreements or advanced financial planning. Our team does these too.

But through a special program which I'll refer to here as "Catapult" (not it's real name so no need to google it), which uses OPM to help fund tax-free cash-flow during retirement (and other needs too) to those with a net worth of just $1,000,000 (exclusive of your home). One IUL accepts a much lower net worth – but I don't like the policy.

If you think about it, wealthy people have always used "leverage" to increase their assets, whether borrowing to purchase or expand a business or buy real estate, etc. They use their borrowing capacity.

Just last week, I was at a conference speaking with a CPA/attorney friend who has been involved with premium financing for his clients for about 15 years. He is now working with a billionaire Wall Street guy and his wife who are looking to finance $400 million of death benefits ($200 million on each) for estate planning purposes. Who would want to write those huge premium checks from their checking account? Nobody – hence the attractiveness of premium financing.

The bank(s) will loan the money to them to pay 100% of the needed premiums, but they will need to post additional collateral (beyond the cash value in the policies) to get the deal done. They will not only be underwritten for their health but also financially (and they'll need to provide annual financial statements to the lenders for as long as the loans are in place). The collateral is still under their control -- earning themselves a return though (the lenders require it "just in case").

Anyway, let's take a quick look at how a Catapult program would look for someone "like most of us" and its advantages over traditional premium finance. In many ways it's actually better than what the multi-millionaires get. For one, the policy is the only collateral needed!

First of all, to qualify for Catapult, you need to be age 65 or under, and be in normal health (without any tobacco/nicotine use for the last 3-5 years). The minimum death benefit is $1.5 million for the maximum-funded contract. It is structured just like any TRIPLE ZERO™ plan. We're simply getting a 3:1 matching premium from bank loans.

You pay about 50% of the premium for only five years. A lender will loan the other 50% or so for those five years. For years 6-10, the bank will pay 100% of the premium and then the policy funding is complete. We then let the cash-value grow with the indexing strategies.

What are the minimum premiums out-of-your-pocket (50% or so) to maximum-fund the Catapult policy? Well, the minimum is based on your age, sex and health to maximum-fund the required $1,500,000 initial death benefit. For example, a 60-year-old male in great health, it would be about $62,000 a year for those five years. For a 50-year-old female in average health, it's about $35,000 a year (for five years only). A 35-year-old male in top health – only about $25,000/year.

Catapult is unique in that there are no loan applications or credit checks – you don't even sign a loan document. However, you still must meet the minimum net worth requirements of the life insurer. They want to be sure it's an appropriate program for you and that you can easily pay your 50% share of the premiums for the first five years.

Why would a bank do that? Because they have 100% collateral in the cash-value of the policy. They are fully protected and can offer a loan rate of something like LIBOR plus 2%. They have virtually zero financial risk and are willing to make these loans all day long. Since about 2004, the company that sponsors the Catapult program (and others) has $4 Billion of premium financing loans on the books (they administer the programs while about 15 top banks are the lenders).

The banks make the program sponsors "stress-test" the policy to the extreme while the loan is outstanding. For bear markets, they test it against the great depression period where 9 of the first 14 years would have earned a zero percent return (the floor). On the other end of the stress-test, they use the high 1980's interest rates and see what that would do to the loan and accrued interest vs. the loan collateral. In both scenarios, the banks are satisfied that their loan is secure, and the collateral of cash-value is enough to offer great loan terms.

Anyway, after the 10 years of policy funding is complete, the cash is then allowed to grow for another five years or so. Although you can decide to walk away from the policy at any time, until the loan and accrued interest is paid off, you cannot use this policy for the Private Reserve strategy since the bank has a first lien on your cash value and death benefit. For some folks that can be a downside to Catapult – no access to your IUL cash until the loan is paid off (anytime) or you decide to exit the plan. But you're already are using leverage – OPM.

If you happen to die during this period, the loan and accrued interest is paid off and your beneficiaries get the full remaining death benefit. But Catapult is designed for you to live a very long time.

In year 15 or so, the cash inside the policy pays off the bank loans. Catapult is built to add from 20% to 35% more tax-free retirement cash-flow than the same policy not using any OPM. That could add $100,000's of more distributions over a long life. On top of all that additional tax-free cash-flow, the protection of the death benefit is much greater from day one -- as well as over the life of the policy. Assuming that over time, the bank loan costs are 1% to 1.5% less than the interest credited to the policy (net of expenses), the benefit of bank loans to leverage your own premium contributions will add an impressive boost to your future invisible retirement cash-flow.

Where do folks get the money to fund their share of the Catapult premiums for the first five years? From several sources (just like any regular TRIPLE ZERO™ plan): discretionary after-tax income, diverting "above the match" contributions from a 401K, use funds in a taxable brokerage account, after-tax cash from a 72(t), etc.

Here's an out-of-the-box thought to dramatically improve the results. Many business owners expect to sell their business 10-15 years in the future. Or real estate owners cashing-out of their properties at some point. Or someone expecting a sizable inheritance. Where do these folks put the proceeds from any of those events to stay out of taxable accounts and get into the never-taxed zone?

You can't put them in a ROTH – or any IRA since they only allow small contributions. You could use those funds to pay the taxes on a ROTH conversion, but you'd likely have a bunch of money left over. How else could you get this money into your Get Me to ZERO™ plan?

Well if it was me, I'd seriously consider paying off the Catapult bank loans... rather than using cash value from inside the policy. That would allow the proceeds from any of the above events to go right into the tax-free zone. Each circumstance would be different, but it wouldn't surprise me that doing this would double the tax-free distributions from the Catapult policy. It would certainly be worth taking a look at.

One final point about Catapult. Catapult has a sister program (let's call it C-Catapult) that looks just like what you've read above. It's for C-Corp businesses and non-profits entities who want to recruit, reward and retain top talent (college coaches, etc.). Or it can even apply to 1099 independent contractors for endorsement deals (think Tiger Woods and Nike). Here's the difference -- instead of the employ<u>ee</u> funding 50% of the premiums for the first five years out of their own pocket, their "employ<u>er</u>" <u>lends</u> them that money instead.

Well, you already know that a loan is not taxable to the employee or contractor, so they are getting untaxed dollars to go into their TRIPLE ZERO™ plan, which after the bank loans will be paid off, will be completely in the zero-tax zone. The employee put none of their own money in this part of their Get Me to ZERO™ strategy – with a huge death benefit to protect their loved ones too. Pretty cool.

And the employer who wanted to give them a "signing bonus" to bring them on the team, or a performance bonus, etc. -- what do they get out of the deal? It's very attractive for them as well as you'll see.

When an employer pays a bonus to an employee, it's an expense. That money is gone forever. But when they make a loan, it becomes an asset (an account receivable) on their balance sheet – that actually earns a little interest (income). Think of it as a 30-40-year bond.

And since that bonus is no longer an expense to the corporation, what just happened to profits? They went up! What happened to the asset side of their balance sheet? There was no financial effect at all.

When does the company get their loan repaid? It's repaid out of part of the death benefit when the employee passes away. Maybe some 30-40 years down the road – but they've been accruing interest along the way. The employee's family gets the rest of the death benefit in addition to all of the tax-free retirement cash-flow they'd get in any TRIPLE ZERO™ or Catapult policy. This is really cool planning.

Ok, we've spent nearly 140 pages explaining why I believe you should strive to pay ZERO income taxes (or as close as possible) in retirement and three powerful strategies to help get you there: ROTH contributions, ROTH conversions and the TRIPLE ZERO™ plan.

But there are a few more strategies that will help all or some of you finish the job, so let's continue with the Get Me to ZERO™ plan.

The 4th Strategy

After reading the last 95 pages or so, one might question why they shouldn't have all their savings in the tax-free zone (anything named ROTH and/or the TRIPLE ZERO™)? Well, if they did that, some might be missing out on something that for many readers, would be a sizeable part of the tax code: the itemized or the standard deduction.

If you recall from the section about the income tax cylinder - where all your taxable income is poured in, there is an "in-between" step before we calculate that some of that income taxed at 10%, some at 12% the next income at 22% and so on. That step is applying itemized deductions such as mortgage interest, real estate taxes, charitable donations, medical expenses, etc. – or use the standard deduction if this figure is larger than the sum of your allowed itemized deductions.

In the new Trump tax law, they bragged about doubling the standard deduction to $12,200 for each spouse. Sounded pretty good. But what you hardly ever heard the politicians talk about was that they eliminated the $4,000 personal exemptions for you and each tax dependent (spouse and kids). Like everything else in the new tax law – there were people who benefited while others lost out. It hurt me and many of my clients. But it is... what it is.

In any case, at $12,200 per tax filer ($24,400 for married filing jointly), millions fewer folks will now itemize their deductions, since the new standard deduction is larger than what it would be with itemizing under the new law. Especially with the "SALT" limits which cap your itemized deductions for all **S**tate **A**nd **L**ocal **T**axes (for both income and real estate taxes) to just $10,000 per return.

And since this book is about retirement income, taxpayers aged 65 and older (or who are blind or disabled) will continue to claim an additional $1,300 each person for married filing jointly ($1,600 for unmarried taxpayers), on top of the standard deduction. That rule remained intact from before the law changed. Therefore, a couple filing jointly that are age 65 or older will have a standard deduction of $27,000 – unless their itemized deductions are greater. You get to deduct the bigger number from your taxable income.

So in effect, without itemizing deductions, the first $27,000 (or $13,800 for unmarried filers) of otherwise taxable income... is tax-free! More, if you itemize. Depending on your total income that would be subject to tax (the lower it is the more meaningful this deduction is), this tax law is an important part of the Get Me to ZERO™ strategy.

But if ALL your income is non-taxable (ROTH and TRIPLE ZERO™ distributions), then you just wasted your standard (or itemized) deductions – since none of that income would even be on your 1040. You'd have no income to use that deduction against. Or would you? For some, it may be OK to still have some IRA money left with RMDs to take advantage of some of this deduction. Those IRA RMDs could be tax-free if they and your Social Security checks were small enough.

But for most of us, Social Security will not be fully tax-free. For those who don't get most of their income to be "invisible" to the tax form, they might pay taxes on up to 85% of those government checks. And that's where this part of the "pay as little taxes as possible" comes in. Wouldn't it be great to pay small taxes on your Social Security checks?

Do you remember the part earlier in the book (page 51) about Provisional income which is the formula for how much of your Social

Security would be subject to tax? Let's revisit that here. As you may recall, ROTH and TRIPLE ZERO™ income do not even show up on the tax returns and are not part of the Provisional Income calculation. That calculation (page 51) includes all earned income, pensions, RMDs or distributions from traditional IRAs, 401Ks, TSPs, etc. PLUS... one-half of your Social Security income. Here's an example.

George and Judy have combined Social Security income of $40,000 per year. They have more income from traditional IRAs that they never converted to ROTHs of about $23,000 and another $25,000/yr. from ROTHs (not meaningful for income taxation purposes). For Provisional income, we use half of their Social Security checks and all their income from traditional IRAs. That gives us $43,000. Since that figure is between $32,000 and $44,000 (filing jointly) only 50% of their Social Security income is going to be subject to tax.

From the $43,000 taxable income, we deduct the standard deduction of $27,000 which leaves $16,000 that is subject to taxes – putting them in the marginal 10% tax rate (see chart on page 35). They'd owe the IRS $1,600 on total retirement cash-flow of $88,000. Their effective tax rate on all that cash-flow is under 2%. Not quite a ZERO tax bill, but pretty darn close. They didn't get to ZERO, but it did make over 82% of their total income tax-free and protected from potential future tax increases.

For comparison sake, let's say that everything was the same, except they never converted any savings to a ROTH. So, they had $48,000 a year in traditional IRA income plus the $40,000 Social Security.

Let's start with Provisional income. We take half of their Social Security ($20,000) and add that to the $48,000 of tax-postponed IRA income and we get $68,000. That is more than $44,000 on the Provisional income chart, so 85% of their Social Security will be subject to tax ($34,000). We'll add the $34,000 to the $48,000 IRA income ($82,000). Let's look at their tax bill under this scenario.

From the $82,000 taxable income, we'll subtract the $27,000 standard deduction - leaving us $55,000 to pay taxes on. We'll pour that income into the tax cylinder and the first $19,400 is taxed at 10% ($1,940) and the next $35,600 will be taxed at 12% ($4,272) for a total tax due to the IRS of $6,212. That's $4,612 more because their large tax-postponed IRAs caused 85% of their Social Security to be subject to tax. That's a 280% larger tax bill (plus state taxes if applicable). They are in the marginal 12% tax bracket, but they paid an effective tax rate of about 7% of their total income. However, they are not protected by potential future income tax hikes?

Here's another example – let's call them Tom and Sue. This couple is getting $60,000 a year in Social Security checks. If all their other income is non-taxed due to the Get Me to ZERO™ plan they put in place, then let's see how this might play out.

Let's say they have just over $1,000,000 in two ROTHs and about $900,000 in their TRIPLE ZERO™ plans (from both a 72(t) and taking withdrawals from a taxable brokerage account to contribute to two IULs) and they are getting $85,000 tax-free from these sources – which besides being in the never-taxed zone, are both non-countable incomes for calculating Provisional income. They're taking $35,000/yr. from the two ROTHs and about $50,000/yr. from the two IULs.

In this example, since the only income that would be subject to the Provisional income formula is Social Security, we use half of that $60,000 figure, which of course is $30,000 for Provisional income.

If you look at the chart on page 51 again, you'll see that a couple filing jointly with Provisional income under $32,000 – NONE of this Social Security income would be subject to tax. So yes, they will pay no federal income taxes that year. Did they waste their $27,000 standard deduction? It wasn't needed to pay ZERO income taxes on $145,000 of retirement cash-flow in this case since they paid their taxes already. But at some point, if their Social Security checks get any COLAs (Cost of Living Adjustments) and grow to have to pay taxes on up to 50% of their Social Security checks, that standard deduction will probably come to their rescue – keeping their federal income taxes as close to ZERO as possible. However, paying no federal income taxes this year on $145,000 of income sounds good to me. Great planning guys!

Again, Tom and Sue never avoided paying any income taxes. They paid the taxes owed on the ROTH conversions and used after-tax money to fund their ROTH 401Ks. They also paid the taxes on the 72(t) from the funds already in their traditional IRAs before putting the premiums into their two TRIPLE ZERO™ policies.

Worried about the prospect of much higher taxes, they simply paid the taxes at a known rate, keeping tax bracket management in mind to avoid jumping into a much higher bracket (from 24% to 32%).

But let's look at what their tax bill would be if the ONLY change to this example was that $50,000 of income came from traditional IRAs (if they did not do a 72(t) from their tax-postponed IRA or move their taxable brokerage account to the tax-free zone of the TRIPLE ZERO™) and still had the $35,000 income from the ROTHs.

That would make their Provisional income go up to $80,000 – putting 85% of their Social Security checks subject to taxation. Which means that $51,000 of their Social security checks would be subject to tax (as well as the $50,000 from the tax-postponed IRAs) for a total of $101,000. From that taxable number, we'll subtract the standard deduction of $27,000, leaving $74,000 subject to tax.

The first $19,400 will be taxed at 10% which equals $1,940. The next $54,600 will be taxed at 12% which comes to $6,552. Tom and Sue's federal tax is not ZERO anymore, it is $8,492. And perhaps state tax and local income taxes too – depending on where they live.

Plus, those tax bills will continue year after year after year for 2-3 decades. And of course, that assumes that tax rates do not go up as

David Walker and so many others believe they will. What if the lowest brackets move from the 10% and 12% today, towards the lowest tax bracket of 25% during the 1960's? What if 22% or 24% goes to 30%?

Again, nobody is avoiding income taxes that they don't already owe to the IRS in the Get Me to ZERO™ strategy. They are just paying taxes on a smaller account balance (instead of the larger one that they hope their investments will grow to) at known rates/brackets/rules and on their own timeline – not the governments. You can be in control.

By the way, with taxable income of $74,000, Tom and Sue are just a few thousand dollars from leaping into the next tax bracket -- 22% on any taxable income over $78,951. Ouch! And what about higher income folks who will likely have much of their retirement income taxed at the 22% and 24% rates (or even higher), would it not make sense to tax-diversify now and get as many of your assets off the IRS's radar screen as possible now, at today's low and known tax rates?

The 5th Potential Strategy

As you've read, most of the heavy lifting in the Get Me to ZERO™ tax strategy is done with the ROTHs and TRIPLE ZERO™s -- avoiding RMDs, while not causing your Social Security to be taxed at the same time. Then, the standard (or itemized) deduction will help many get closer to paying little or no income taxes during retirement.

The fifth strategy is one, that without a bit more education, you may dismiss it right away -- based on outdated or just plain wrong information. But I think you should at least be aware of it and knowledgeable enough to decide if it may be right for you to consider in striving to pay ZERO taxes in retirement and simultaneously add a great deal of strategic and financial flexibility to your life.

The fifth strategy is called a Reverse Mortgage. These products have become better and better (due to the Reverse Mortgage Stabilization

Act of 2013) and are certainly much more consumer friendly. Well-known academic researchers (like Dr. Wade Pfau, author of "Reverse Mortgages" book) and many other savvy advisors have touted their usefulness and flexibility in retirement income planning.

For one, the new FHA regulations have eliminated the risk that a non-borrower spouse could be forced out of the home at the death of the borrower spouse. Dr. Pfau also noted that the perception that the borrower loses the title to the home when he or she takes out a reverse mortgage is another complete myth.

Another possible obstacle to using reverse mortgages is the stigma over taking on debt, especially if you've finally paid off your mortgage. Dr. Pfau said there is "probably a better way to frame reverse mortgages". When someone spends money from their retirement portfolio, they don't think of it as debt and Dr. Pfau said spending from home equity can be viewed the same way. "You have to compensate for that through paying back the loan balance, but the home is the collateral on that loan, so you're really just spending down your home in the same way you might spend down your investment portfolio." That explanation makes sense.

The problem with most advisors, TV financial "celebrities" and even consumers who categorically refuse to even consider this financial tool, is that they are living in the past. They do not know... what they do not know. They have not kept up with their financial education.

As I've always said, no financial tool is right for every situation. Each and every single product or service in any industry has its pros and cons. Nothing is perfect, but a new reverse mortgage offers very flexible options to solve many retirement problems.

According to a LIMRA study, in 1989 only 11% of homeowners aged 65-74 carried a mortgage into their retirement. At that time, the average mortgage balance for these people was about $29,000.

Things are very different today. Almost 44% of people in this age group have a mortgage and the average balance is nearly $137,000.

There are three main ways that a reverse mortgage could potentially add value to your retirement (in no particular order).

#1: For some folks, I recommend using a reverse mortgage to pay-off the balance owed on their primary home mortgage. Why consider this? Because if you do not have a monthly mortgage payment (the principal and interest portion), then you do not need as much income to enjoy the same exact tax-free lifestyle. You get to live in the same house (for as long as either of you want to) with no more principal and interest payments (which may not be deductible anymore if you use the standard deduction rather than itemizing).

Yes, you'll still have to pay your real estate taxes, HOA dues, homeowners' insurance, and maintain the property, but that will always be the case whether your home has a traditional mortgage, a reverse mortgage or it is fully paid-off. So, in that respect, your ongoing lifestyle (housing accommodation) is the same. But you just reduced your after-tax monthly cost to live... the way you'd like to.

#2: Other clients (with their home all or substantially paid-for) can open a HECM reverse mortgage. They get an open line of credit to access the funds whenever they need or want to. And of course, funds accessed from a reverse mortgage are TAX-FREE. Just like a ROTH distribution or a properly-made distribution from TRIPLE ZERO™ policy, funds from a reverse mortgage will not cause taxation of your Social Security or increase your Medicare premiums (IRMMA).

Let me give you an example of a 65-year-old couple whose home is valued at $300,000 and is paid for. At the time of writing this section, they could establish a reverse mortgage line of credit (HECM) of about $125,000. They would have a small amount of closing costs to open that "standby" line of credit, but they would not owe any loan interest until they accessed the credit line. There are no monthly payments at all, however they have immediate access to capital if they need it.

For a couple of thousand dollars of closing costs (with the right mortgage company -- they are not all the same), I think this is money well spent. Think of it as an insurance policy to protect your home's current value (remember what happened to real estate values in the last recession when many homes lost 30%-50% in value).

If untouched, in ten years that $125,000 line of credit may grow to $185,000 for future use. In 20 and 30 years it may grow to $270,000 and $400,000 respectively. Both the growth of the line of credit and interest rates charged on any loans are variable and property value decreases cannot affect your credit line (unlike a regular home equity line from a bank, the HECM cannot be closed or shut-off).

That's an important fact: a HECM line of credit is also a nice hedge against falling house values. Once your line of credit is open, unlike a traditional HELOC, it cannot be decreased or closed by the bank – EVER. As stated, it grows each year when left untouched.

If your home is worth $600,000 and your age is 66, current interest rates allow a $260,000 HECM. As stated, if we have another housing crisis like in the late 2000's, that line of credit figure is protected!

Why open the reverse mortgage HECM now if you don't need the tax-free funds today? As stated, the line of credit will increase over time (based on a formula – not appreciation) and it will be available immediately should you ever need the cash. This principal limit growth formula will almost always allow for greater access to funds later in retirement than if you wait to open the reverse mortgage until later when it may be first needed or wanted to take advantage of. VITAL to Know: Besides the value of your home, in determining the maximum amount of a reverse mortgage you can get, it is NOT your age(s) that is the biggest factor... it is current interest rates. The lower interest rates are, the higher the potential line of credit that can be available. If mortgage rates are going to continue to rise, now is an optimal time to explore opening a HECM line of credit.

The size of the reverse mortgage is essentially based on a present value calculation. The lower the discount rate, the lower the interest rate, the higher the present value and the bigger available loan size.

You could access the line of credit in lieu of your ROTHs that are invested in the stock markets when its crashing, rather than selling those investments that have dropped in value to pay for your living expenses. That way, you can give your ROTHs the time to recover.

Other potential uses are to tap the reverse mortgage equity line to use as income while delaying filing for your Social Security benefits (the longer you wait the bigger the monthly SS check) and allow your other investment accounts grow too. One can also take a monthly tax-free income from the reverse mortgage to reduce their portfolio withdrawal rate and sequence of returns risk (explained later).

You should know that FHA reverse mortgages are non-recourse loans which means, that you or your heirs can never owe more than the home is worth – even if the loan becomes larger than the home's value. That old "worry" continues to be a big myth too! If the home is worth more than the outstanding loan balance when the home is sold, then you or your heirs get to keep the rest of any equity.

The home must be your primary residence and you must own the home outright or use the proceeds of the reverse mortgage to pay off their existing mortgage. The youngest borrower must be at least age 62. Although, a non-borrowing spouse may be younger than age 62.

Many financial advisors (including myself) used to hold back the reverse mortgage as a "Plan B". But I've learned that is not the best advice. The best general advice is to open up the HECM line of credit earlier rather than later and let it grow until (if ever) it is needed.

The only caveat to this strategy of opening a HECM now may be if you don't plan on staying in your primary home for at least 5-7 years. If you plan on moving elsewhere within that timeframe, you may want to consider waiting to set up a reverse mortgage until you get in a more permanent home and avoid the costs of opening a 2nd HECM.

#3: Speaking of moving into a new home, another way to use a reverse mortgage is to "downsize without downsizing"… OR get twice the new house for about half the price. Let me explain this second idea with an example situation who I thought this made perfect sense.

A gentleman just retired from the federal government and planned on selling his condo in Atlanta and move to Sarasota, FL. He told me that he had a champagne desire on a beer budget (not really the case as he had plenty of pension, Social Security and investment income).

As I recall, he thought he'd net about $275,000 for his condo and didn't want to spend more than perhaps $300,000 for the perfect place in Sarasota. I suggested that he could afford (using a reverse mortgage) to purchase a dream $450,000 home using just the proceeds from his condo sale – and not have a monthly mortgage payment from a traditional mortgage. He could have and enjoy his "Champaign home" for the price of beer.

For him, there is no downside. If this was my own personal situation, I'd do it in a heartbeat. He is single and has no children to leave a home to. Should he pass away or go to an LTC facility down the road, he (or his heirs) can sell the property and pay off the reverse mortgage and receive any remaining equity. If the home is worth less than the loan balance, they can walk away and give the FHA the keys.

But nonetheless, can you imagine the possibilities to improve the rest of his life! This may be a good strategy for you too. Or maybe not.

Again, no financial tool is perfect or right for everyone, but a reverse mortgage can incorporate your home equity into improving your overall retirement income & tax strategy. Having said all of that, you should know that there are still abuses in the reverse mortgage market. Some mortgage brokers are selling some people a mortgage that is not in their best interest. Or one with maximum costs and fees.

And please, NEVER use the proceeds from a reverse mortgage to make an "investment" in anything. Not an IUL, not an annuity or a mutual fund or anything. That is a regulatory RED FLAG in my business.

Costs of reverse mortgages vary widely, and comparison shopping could save you thousands of dollars. Borrowers should consider different combinations of both upfront costs as well as future interest rates on the loan. A reverse mortgage specialist's advice is critical!

Although I do not personally market (nor am I licensed to do so) reverse mortgages (nor do I get any kickbacks, fees, commissions or any other type of compensation from reverse mortgages), our group does have a special deal with one of the top reverse mortgage specialists in the country. That team specializes in this niche market and can save our clients substantial costs. Of course, I would still encourage you to shop around and compare so you can make the smartest decision for you. Ok, enough on reverse mortgages.

Before we go to the sixth strategy, what's the real reason to strive to Get Me to ZERO™? To be frank, it's to enhance your financial life – both NOW... and during retirement. Saving up to $300,000 or more of taxes is wonderful. Having access to your cash to work in two places at once is too. So is avoiding big market losses. But there's more. The point of this book is to show you how to gain a better life. That's what counts. How to make the most of your financial resources and take full advantage of your opportunities and longstanding tax laws. The "how" is just a means to an end. The "end" is to simply ensure a better, less stressful life. To be in more control. To live life... on your own terms.

The 6th Strategy

December 2015 was an important month for all charitably minded Americans. It was that month that the U.S. Congress passed a new law, allowing you to give up to $100,000 to a charity directly from your traditional IRA when you are over 70½ years old (satisfying your RMD) – and here's the key -- without adding the distribution to your Adjusted Gross Income. This type of charitable gift is called a Qualified Charitable Distribution (QCD). And hardly anybody is talking about it!

And this law survived the Trump tax changes! So, for people with charitable intentions, who are required to take RMDs from traditional IRAs that were never converted to ROTHs (which have no RMDs), this could be a sixth strategy to help Get Me to ZERO™.

As you know, when you take money out of your IRA it is a taxable event. The distribution adds income to your tax cylinder and raises your Adjusted Gross Income (AGI) and provisional income. Then, if you donate the same amount to your charity, the charitable gift reduces your taxable income by the amount of the donation -- but that gift does not reduce your Provisional Income or AGI.

However, if you use a QCD, rather than take a typical withdrawal, it is not taxable income, it doesn't really show up on your tax return and it has no effect whatsoever on your AGI. Therefore, a QDC will not cause your Social Security income to be taxed nor can it increase your Medicare Part B and D premiums as a normal RMD could.

Millions of Americans over age 70½ who are required to take RMDs also give to their church or place of worship. Many folks tithe 10% of their income. Some give much more to charities and causes that they care deeply about. A QDC can be a much more tax savvy way to give.

But with the new tax law, unless their giving and the total of their other deductions are larger than the standard deduction, they'd pay more in taxes than they should. They'd get no tax benefit for the donation they've made to charity. A QDC can help fix that issue.

Giving to a charity or religious organization directly from your IRA allows you to ignore your QCD IRA distribution when calculating your taxable income and take the standard deduction at the same time.

For big donors, charitable giving can only be deducted if it is less than 50% of your AGI. But donating directly from your IRA using a QDC allows you to effectively reduce your AGI (up to the $100,000 per year limit) even if the gift amount would otherwise be greater than 50% of your AGI.

All QCDs count as IRA distributions and can be used to satisfy all or just a part of your annual RMD. This makes them particularly useful for older retirees who may be still working (earned income), not wanting their Social Security to be taxed, have a large pension, or may be able to get to or stay in a lower tax bracket by using the QDC.

There are 3 easy hurdles to qualify for a QCD:

1. A QCD must come from a Traditional IRA (or an Inherited IRA) where the owner is over 70½. QCDs can never be made from any work-based retirement accounts such as 401Ks, TSPs, 403Bs, a Simple IRA or a SEP IRA. Those accounts must be first rolled over into an IRA.

2. The IRA distribution must transfer directly from your IRA to a Qualified Charity which includes all IRS 501(c)(3) organizations such as churches, schools, the Red Cross, Cancer Society, etc. However, that list excludes all foundations, donor-advised funds (DAFs) and some others. Make sure you verify that the organization fully qualifies.

3. You must receive a letter of confirmation from the charity. The letter must include the statement that no goods or services were received by you in exchange (no quid pro quo) for the charitable donation. That is normal procedure to get any charitable deduction on your tax return when you itemize.

To sum this strategy up, QCDs are typically most beneficial for people with money still held in Traditional IRAs and who do not need all of their annual RMD funds to enjoy their desired lifestyle and of course, who would otherwise give to their favorite charity(s) and who will not find it beneficial to itemize deductions.

In some circumstances, some charitably-minded retirees might get more tax savings by making donations of highly appreciated stock in their taxable brokerage accounts than by employing QCDs. Such stock donations experience double tax savings. Not only does a gift of low-basis stocks count as a tax deduction, thereby reducing taxable income, but also that donation also avoids paying federal capital gains tax (and perhaps state tax) that would have been owed had you simply sold the stock. But QCDs can be a powerful tool.

The 7th Strategy

The seventh strategy for the Get Me to ZERO™ goal is actually four general ideas below plus a list of 15 very effective miscellaneous tax-saving strategies that may help you slash your taxes in retirement or maybe right now – especially for business owners and the wealthy! Most of the 15 will not be applicable to you. But you never know...

1) The first one I'll write about is Municipal bonds (bonds issued by states, counties and cities, etc.). I'm sure there are several readers that are wondering why I haven't used them as an 8th strategy since interest from muni bonds are not taxed at the federal level. That's true. And the interest from a muni bond issued in the state you live will also be tax-free. But that's only part of the story.

Any and all interest from muni bonds go into the Provisional Income calculation and can cause your Social Security income to be taxed. Yes, that's true. Even though you won't pay federal income taxes on muni bond interest, they could cause you to pay taxes on your Social Security and can also increase your Medicare Part B and D premiums.

You should also know that should muni bonds increase in value (with interest rates dropping or improvements in credit ratings) and if you sell your bonds, there is a capital gains tax to be paid to the IRS. And interest from muni bonds issued in another state may be taxable to you on your state tax returns. If you live in a state with dubious finances, you'd likely want to own your muni bonds from more credit-worthy states which could be subject to taxation in your own state.

Here's another reason why I didn't include muni bonds as one of the main ways to pay as little taxes in retirement as possible. Normally only the very wealthy should even consider them because when you compare taxable bonds rates to muni rates, you usually have to be in the highest tax brackets for them to make any sense at all. Historically, muni bonds have lower yields than taxable corporate bonds.

Here's a financial formula that will help you determine whether to invest in taxable or tax-free bonds is the calculation of the "taxable equivalent yield". This is the interest rate you would need to earn from a taxable bond to generate the same after-tax yield as a tax-free muni bond. Simply calculate the taxable equivalent yield by dividing the tax-free yield by 1 minus your marginal income tax bracket. For example, if you are in the federal 22 percent tax bracket, a 3% tax-free yield is divided by .78 to give a taxable bond equivalent yield of 3.84%.

Keep in mind that for a couple to hit the 22% marginal tax bracket, they need over $78,951 of taxable income (after subtracting their itemized deductions or the $24,400 stand deduction) which would put them over $103,000 of gross income.

Of course, another consideration in deciding between taxable and tax-free bonds, is to compare bonds with similar credit ratings and time to maturity. In the example above, I'm assuming these metrics are comparable to each other. And don't forget that if you have moved most or all of your funds to ROTHs or TRIPLE ZERO™ plans – income taxes no longer matter! I love the sound of those last 5 words.

If you are in the 12% marginal tax bracket because you took to heart the strategies in this book, then a muni bond would not likely be a wise choice (plus the potential effect on Social Security taxation).

One final point about bonds in general at this stage of the economic cycle. Bonds have been in a 30+ year bull market with interest rates coming down since the 1980's. But now, many economists think this trend is reversing, and interest rates will continue to rise over time.

Prices of bonds and interest rates are generally inverse, meaning when interest rates rise, the price of bonds will fall. Therefore, bond prices are facing an uphill battle if interest rates continue to rise over the next number of years. Not a good problem in retirement.

Personally, I'm not in the camp that thinks interest rates will rise dramatically over the next few years. But failing another recession, I think "total returns" from all bonds (taxable and muni) will struggle to keep up with real inflation. In my opinion, there are better places to put money that are not as interest rate sensitive and will act as a portfolio's ballast to more volatile stocks. Roger Ibbotson of the asset-allocation research firms agrees. I'll explain more in a later chapter.

2) I've written about Social Security and Provisional income. Even with no Get Me to ZERO™ planning at all, no more than 85% of your Social Security checks will be subject to taxation. That means at least 15% will be tax-free under current federal law.

For a couple with combined Social Security income of $40,000 a year – that means at least $6,000 will not be taxed at all. I'd rather that none of it was taxed after using ROTHs and TRIPLE ZERO™s, but one needs to take action to put yourself in that wonderful position.

3) Health Savings Accounts (HSAs). Health Savings Accounts (were created in 2003 so that individuals/families covered by high-deductible health insurance plans could receive tax-preferred treatment of

money saved for future medical expenses. Generally, an adult who is covered by a high-deductible health plan (and has no other first-dollar coverage) may establish an HSA. To qualify in 2019, minimum annual deductibles are $1,350 for self-only coverage or $2,700 for family coverage (no change from 2018).

HSA holders can choose to save up to $3,500/yr. for an individual and $7,000/yr. for a family (HSA holders 55 and older get to save an extra $1,000 which means $4,500 for an individual and $8,000 for a family) in an HSA account. There's those government limits again! HSA contributions are 100% tax deductible from gross income (like a traditional IRA) however when used for qualifying health care expenses, the withdrawals are 100% tax-free (like a ROTH). Interest earned in the HSA also compounds tax-deferred (no 1099's). Great!

So, the HSA contributions are tax-deductible today, interest is tax-deferred and when withdrawn for qualifying medical expenses, are 100% tax-free. Pretty sweet deal. The only problems are, you need to have a high-deductible insurance plan (private or at work) and as you saw above, the amount you can contribute each year is pretty low.

HSA withdrawals will not count as Provisional Income nor cause your Social Security to be taxed or increase your Medicare premiums.

However, any funds you withdraw from an HSA for non-qualified medical expenses will always be taxed at your marginal income tax rate, plus a 10% tax penalty (unless you are age 65 or older, become totally and permanently disabled or die).

One thing that I can be pretty sure of is that most folks are going to have big out-of-pocket health care expenses during their retirement. Either co-pays, deductibles, uncovered medical expenses and so on.

So if funding an HSA is an option for you. I'd seriously consider jumping on it. Every little bit helps in beating the IRS at their game.

Pay them less. Keep more money for yourself and have a better life!

Again, if you think taxes are going to have to rise dramatically due to the $22 Trillion of U.S. debt, trillions more in unfunded liabilities like Social Security, Medicare, Medicaid, etc. then it's in your best interest to legally avoid as much future taxation as you can.

Politicians from both parties, Democrats and Republicans keep kicking the "financial can" down the road. It can't disappear, but they can push the fiscal problems down to our children and grandchildren.

Any logical thinking person realizes that a government that keeps putting spending on the "national credit card", must have a day of reckoning at some point. And that reckoning will be higher taxes for either ourselves and/or generations to come. But ignoring the problem won't make it go away. But we can take measures to protect ourselves. Anyway, let's get back to our next strategy...

4) Here's a potentially big one that the new Trump tax law did not take away. If you're a homeowner this is the one tax law you need to thoroughly understand so you can avoid paying capital gains taxes on the sale of your primary residence for up to $500,000 in profits for a married couple filing jointly (and up to $250,000 for single filers).

By profits, I mean the sale proceeds over and above your adjusted basis. For example, if you bought your primary home for $350,000 back in 2001 and added $100,000 of improvements over time, your adjusted basis is now $450,000. If you sell it for $850,000 today, you will not have to pay capital gains taxes on the $400,000 profit if you are married and filing jointly. If you are a single filer, the first $250,000 of those profits would be tax-free and you'd owe taxes on $150,000.

And if you qualify for that capital gains tax exclusion, you may do whatever you'd like with the tax-free proceeds from the sale of your primary home. Anything – but from now on, it's in the taxable bucket.

You are not required to reinvest the proceeds in another home. But, if you do buy another house, you can qualify for the exclusion again when you sell that home. In fact, you can use the primary home exclusion many times over your lifetime -- as long as you satisfy the requirements detailed below. But you may not use this special tax break more than once every two years.

In order for the sale to qualify, the homeowner(s) must own and use the home as their primary residence for at least 2 of the past 5 years. For a married couple, the requirement is satisfied as long as either spouse owns the home, though both must use it as their primary residence to qualify for the full $500,000 joint exclusion.

Notably, the use of the home does not have to be the last 2 years, just any of the past 2-in-5 years that the property was owned. Under some circumstances there can be some pro-rata time rules too.

The two-year rule is really generous, since most people live in their home at least that long before they sell it. (Americans move once every seven years on average). By wisely using the exclusion in the years leading up to and throughout retirement, you can buy and sell many homes over the years and avoid any income taxes on your profits. Again, always get professional tax advice beforehand.

Because the exclusion is available as often as once every 2 years, some savvy homeowners may even try to sell and move and upgrade homes frequently and continue to take advantage of one capital gains exclusion after another on progressively better homes. Of course, that presumes that home prices will continue to rise. They may not.

Some people even sell their primary home and then move into a vacation rental property they have owned for a while and live there for two years before selling it (and avoiding the capital gains tax again) There are some complications with that strategy that may diminish it somewhat, so please consult with your qualified tax advisor.

This may not be the right potential strategy combination for you, but imagine for a moment cashing out of your primary residence and using the $500,000/$250,000 capital gains tax exclusion. And then using a reverse mortgage to buy your permanent retirement home – getting twice the home for about half the price and pocketing the cash difference to enjoy an even better retirement.

There are many other strategies in Get Me to ZERO™ planning to delay, decrease and avoid income taxation such as 1031 tax-free RE exchanges, HRAs, PR 20/22, CLLCs, ESOPs, step-up in basis, Cost Segs, MIS's, depreciation, O-Z's, Captives, Conservation Easements, gifting, RPTs, multi-entity planning, etc., etc., but they are not applicable to everyone. If they make sense for a client, I'll bring that concept up, educate them to the pros and cons and then make a recommendation.

Before moving on to matters pertaining on how to possibly invest your ROTHs to lower your risk and answer likely questions about IULs and TRIPLE ZERO™ plans, I'd like to address one fairly common issue millions may face in the Get Me to ZERO™ strategy – pension income.

Pension Income

Pensions as a source of retirement income are getting rarer and rarer for folks 5-10 years from retirement – except for federal and other government employees. Some of these folks will have Social Security income as well as their pension, others will not.

Unless you have a lump sum option with your pension (which you may decide to convert to a ROTH) getting to ZERO is probably going to be impossible for you. But using the strategies in this book, at least you can keep your federal income tax burden as low as possible – maybe in the 12% marginal bracket instead of at 22% or higher.

For those of you who have a lump sum option, like everything else in this world, there are pros and cons to taking that... or the promised monthly payout for life – with or without survivorship benefits.

A pension is just a promise to pay. Some of those promises will be kept in full. You'll have to decide if your monthly pension will be safe or if you should take the lump sum. But here's the truth about many of the pension plans that so many Americans are counting on.

The Government Accountability Office (GAO) has continued to warn current and future retirees that the Pension Benefit Guaranty Corp.'s (PBGC) financial assistance to multi-employer plans continues to increase, threatening the financial solvency of the fund and therefore, its financial guarantees to those retirees. Think of the PBGC as similar to what the FDIC is to banks – an added level of protection but with much less financial strength, backing or power.

The Guarantee fund is supposed to cover and provide a minimum retirement income guarantee to more than 40 million workers and retirees. But since 2009, PBGC's financial assistance to the troubled retirement plans has increased dramatically, primarily because of a growing number of pension plan insolvencies.

These pension plan insolvencies were caused by both very poor investment management and returns plus way too low levels of contributions to the pension plan from the employer.

By 2017, the PBGC expects the number of pension insolvencies to more than double, which will further stress the insurance fund. PBGC officials said that financial assistance to retirement pension plans that are insolvent or "are likely to become insolvent in the next 10 years" would likely exhaust the insurance fund within the next 10-15 years.

If the PBGC insurance fund is exhausted, many retirees will see their benefits reduced to a small fraction of their original value because only a reduced stream of current insurance premium payments will be available to pay income benefits to retirees.

According to MSN Money, nearly 80% of the private pension plans covered by the PBGC are underfunded by a total of some $740 billion. That's nearly three-quarters of a TRILLION dollars' worth of promises made that are not likely to be fully kept. The news is just as bad among the nation's largest companies. It's hard to believe, but only 18 pension plans offered by companies that are part of the S&P 500 index are fully-funded and secure. To me, that's inexcusable.

That works out to less than 4% of the biggest public companies in America that are financially ready to keep their full promises for their employee's retirement. That's so pitiful and most folks have absolutely no idea how bad it is and how potentially perilous their retirement may be. These folks think they are set for life. I hope it works out.

According to the PBGC, over 1,400 companies shut down their pension plans in fiscal year 2011, compared with 1,200 in during 2009. An additional 152 pension plans failed (meaning they were terminated without enough money to pay promised benefits) and were taken over by the PBGC.

Again, the PBGC itself, which is funded by employer-paid insurance premiums, is running a $79 billion accumulated deficit. It is being held together by "duct tape" in the eyes of many people in-the-know.

I've mentioned how under-funded most government pension funds are here as well. And the PBGC does NOT cover these types of pension funds. Most government pensions, including the federal government, do not offer a lump sum option. So, there can't be a ROTH conversion.

There are hundreds of towns, cities, counties and even some states that have promised more than they will likely be able to deliver to both past and current employees. If you are fortunate enough to have earned a federal pension you should have fewer worries as they can just print more money. But those pension promises could change! There's already been talk of removing COLAs, etc. to save money.

According to a 2016 report by the Pew Charitable Trusts, public pension funds (cities, towns, counties and states) are underfunded by $1.4 Trillion, up $295 Billion from 2015. To begin to close that funding gap, 35 states have reduced pension benefits for their employees, and half have dramatically increased worker contributions to their plans.

Three forward-thinking states -- Georgia, Michigan and Utah – and 1,000's of municipalities have implemented what is called "hybrid plans" that include defined contribution plans (which are similar to 401Ks), that shift more investment and longevity risk to their workers. Expect more and more public pension funds to follow that lead.

The bottom line is that even though you are "counting" on a company or government pension (or even a company or government retirement health plan) in the years to come, you might consider figuring out how secure that "promise" will be (and a promise is all that it really is). Any pension plan or health plan can be frozen, shut down or altered, changing how much you can expect in retirement.

To find out how secure or underfunded your own pension plan is, simply request that information from your HR department and carefully READ and review the annual benefit and funding statements that your plan is required by law to provide every year -- so you can gauge its financial health. Anything below 80% funding is cause for real concern and perhaps a very good reason to seriously look at taking a lump sum (and run!) if it's offered.

Taking a lump sum has its pros and cons too. You can control the investment and perhaps enjoy more investment control and have potential inflation protection (many pension income amounts are fixed for life). Or you could take the lump sum (convert to a ROTH?) and then buy a guaranteed annuity income stream from an insurance company which is likely in much better financial shape than your employer. I would certainly caution against taking a lump sum and putting it in the stock market – with no guarantees whatsoever!

For pension replacement, many of my clients choose some type of annuity due to better guarantees, the potential for rising income most years, to keep control of and access to their principal and be able to leave a substantial balance to loved ones should they pass-on early. As mentioned, the other opportunity that taking a lump sum in lieu of lifetime monthly payments, is that you can convert all or part of these funds to a ROTH and get it out of the forever-taxed bucket and put it in the never-again taxed bucket.

Certainly, everyone's situation is different, and you should seek advice from a highly qualified and experienced financial advisor.

Ok, we've looked at seven strategies to help Get Me to ZERO™ or at least pay as little federal and state income taxes as possible under both longstanding tax law and the changes made under the new Trump tax law. I certainly hope that you found these strategies both interesting and eye-opening. If you think taxes have got to go higher over the next 10-25 years, using them can materially improve your retirement. Even if your taxes don't go up (not sure how that would happen) there are so many other financial benefits. Pay the IRS less. You keep more and have a better life.

For the rest of the book, I'll write about risk and volatility in your ROTHs and traditional IRAs (and brokerage accounts). Saving taxes is important, but that assumes you don't lose much of your life savings to bear markets and recessions -- or lose the battle against inflation -- especially if you or your spouse live for a long time without paychecks from work. I'll also provide some ideas that I use in my own practice.

After that, I'll answer what I'm sure will be some of your initial questions about the TRIPLE ZERO™ plans. As previously stated, more pages were devoted to this subject in the book since relatively few folks know much about this topic. And quite frankly, there is a tremendous amount of lies, misconceptions and half-truths about IULs on the internet. I'll give you the facts that can be proven.

Sequence of Returns Risk

As I update this book in Dec. 2018, the outlook isn't particularly rosy for people that are on the verge of retiring in the next year or two (or three). And the reason that many financial planners have that worry for clients now is a concept called "Sequence of Returns" risk.

Mutual fund company Thornburg Investment Management defines sequence of return risk this way: "Sequence of returns is simply the order in which returns are realized by a retiree. The consequences of a bad sequence of returns, especially early in retirement, can mean premature depletion of the portfolio. Retirees need to avoid being in the position of having to sell during inopportune market environments."

In other words, market performance in the first five or so years of retirement can determine one's financial security for the remainder of their life. A client retiring right before a bear market can be taking withdrawals in a market spiraling downward. Those withdrawn funds are no longer there to ever recover with an eventual market rebound.

Retiring in late 2007, with the market headed downward for about 18 months (-50% from peak to trough loss), would be a tough hurdle to handle for a 20 or 30+ year retirement. That is of course, unless the actual withdrawals from your stock portfolio were dramatically reduced (and your lifestyle) to coincide with falling markets.

And Sequence of Returns risk can be just as damaging during long periods of mediocre market returns. From 2000-2011 the S&P 500 had an average annual rate of return of just +0.57%. (By the way, a TRIPLE ZERO™ plan had an average annual ROR of +5.1% with a 12% cap.)

The CAPE ratio (the Shiller Cyclically Adjusted P/E ratio) is often cited as a good predictor of real returns over a decade or more. The CAPE ratio started 2018 at a value of roughly 33 – which is higher than it was before the bear markets of 2008 and 1929 (and close to the number in 2000). A high CAPE ratio has preceded the last two bad bear markets this century. Of course, that doesn't mean a bear market is right around the corner – but to some, it can signal caution ahead.

Dan Blanchett, Head of Retirement research at Morningstar, said in an article from the May 7, 2018 Investment News magazine, "There hasn't been a point in the last 140 years... were the CAPE ratio has been this high and bond yields this low. Going back to 1870, the average 10-year US Treasury yield has been 4.6%. Today, it's about 3%" (about double from the 1.4% yield a year or so ago).

In my Retirement Income Planning book, I give an example of Sequence of Returns risk with a brother and sister retiring just 3 years apart with the same size savings invested in the S&P 500 and the same level of withdrawals. The brother retired in 1996 with the first three years of returns in the double digits. His sister retired in 1999, right before the nearly -50% drop of the markets in 2000, 2001 and 2002.

The brother's retirement timing turned out great. His account was 50% bigger after 15 years of withdrawals. His sister's total account value was down about -75% after only 12 years of withdrawals.

Below is a chart from YahooFinance.com of Japan's Nikkei 225 index (their S&P 500) from 1989 to 2017. Back then, Japan was the world's 2nd largest economy after the USA. Today it's number three after the USA and China. It's still a huge economy.

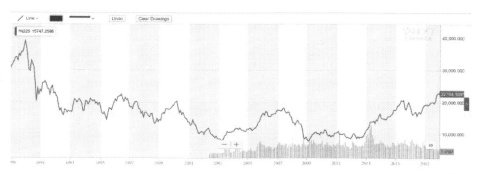

In 1989, their stock market peaked at near 40,000. That was over 29 years ago and it has never been close to that mark since. At the end of 2018, it was still under 21,000, lower than it was in 1996. The #1 song in that year was: "Macarena" by Los Del Rio – (Bayside Boys Mix)!

This is an extreme (but factual) example of Sequence of Returns risk. Investors in Japan have never even gotten close to becoming whole. Imagine newly retirees in 1989 there trying to spend their dwindling savings over the rest of their lives. In about 2003, the Nikkei 225 index finally hit about 9,000 at its low – a 75% drop over about 14 years.

I'm certainly not proposing anything like what happened in Japan will happen in the USA. We are the greatest country in the world. But this chart does prove that unlike our normal regular bear markets and subsequent recoveries, there is no law of economics that say markets must ever recover... or even recover on any particular timetable.

Whether it's a time period of near all-time market highs like 1999 or 2007, Sequence of Returns is a real risk to folks about ready to retire. The problem is, nobody can know for sure when the next 2008 is going to happen and plan their retirement timing accordingly. So, what can you do, to reduce or perhaps even eliminate your risk of being on the "wrong" side of the sequence of returns during your first years of taking retirement income withdrawals? More proactive investing.

2 Buckets of Risk

Before I discuss the topic of market risk, let me write a few words on my observing the general public and investing, based on my 20 years of working with prospective clients from across the country. I'm sure many of my professional peers would back my observations up as well.

We've all heard about the studies showing that the vast majority of us consider ourselves to be above average drivers. Psychologists call this belief "positive illusion". Humans are positive illusion factories!

Positive illusions are a form of self-deception in which humans have inflated, overly-optimistic attitudes about themselves. There are two general types of thinking that are a common cognitive bias in our own positive illusions. The first is an over-estimation of one's special abilities, skills, gifts, traits, powers and successes. Most folks tend to mentally emphasize their good qualities and underestimate the prevalence of their not-so-good abilities and traits at the same time.

For example, only 50% of drivers can actually be above average, yet according to a study published in a Swedish Psychology journal (*Acta Psychologica*) "a whopping 93% of Americans considered themselves above average drivers". That's just not statistically possible.

This phenomenon doesn't just occur with driving, but with just about each area of our life. Whether it's judging our IQ, our athletic prowess, work ethic, health, rating our popularity compared others, or judging how well we get along with others (one study shows 25% of people believe they are in the top 1% of "how easy they think they get along with others, compared to their peers").

So the pertinent positive illusion for this book is one's view of their own investment ability. For 25 years, the DALBAR studies clearly show that the average investor has underperformed the markets (both equities and fixed income) by a wide margin. Is your own investing ability really above average? In the top 25%? Not really sure? Are you willing to bet your retirement lifestyle on it? Is your spouse willing to make that same bet as well? Would you consider acknowledging the "past performance" disclaimer for your own investment results too?

The second type of positive illusion is an overestimation of the amount of control someone has in a particular situation. Some folks have the tendency to believe they have control over outcomes that they in fact, have no influence over whatsoever. This can be seen in gambling, where people use tricks and superstitious behaviors - believing these will influence the outcomes of "games of chance".

An example here would be the future sequence of returns. Or future tax rates and brackets. Future inflation or health care costs. COLAs on your Social Security checks. Another would be how long you (or our spouse) will live? Will one of you need long-term care (LTC)?

Ok, back to the risk buckets as they might relate to the Get Me to ZERO™ strategy. Readers of my other books will know about the 3 buckets of risk, but as my practice has evolved over time, so has my thinking on describing market risk. I now see it as black and white. The money is either at risk of loss due to the markets... or it isn't.

Yes, there are really 3 basic risk buckets: Principal Protected, Lower Risk (like fixed income) and Higher Risk (Stocks). And because of the way my old firm managed money (with money managers that would go to cash when markets were trending lower, they avoided much of the losses in 2008) they called their 3rd risk bucket: Moderate Risk.

But as that firm improved their investment methodology for their clients, what I've come to see as just TWO risk buckets all along, they are now seeing it the same way: 1) "Principal Protected" bucket (no market risk at all) and 2) "Managed Assets" (money exposed to the stock and bond markets which do have inherent risk no matter who is managing them). Whether you use active management, tactical, index or passive investing, there is always market risk in bucket #2. Period.

According to Inc. Magazine, my new firm is one of the fastest-growing private companies in the U.S. We've managed this success by offering investors innovative portfolio strategies and a proven system for simplifying investing. Using Tactical Asset Allocation, when market cycles change and it's most prudent to move to safe-haven assets, our models don't hesitate to proactively reallocate funds away from harm rather than the traditional "buy, hold, hope... and pray" investing.

For bucket #2, Tactical Asset Allocation is becoming more popular as investors prefer a methodology that strives to protect from market downside while still participating in market upside. This is especially true within the five years immediately before retirement and the first 5-10 years of withdrawals. This is the Retirement Red Zone.

Almost every investor is familiar with the aforementioned disclaimer required to be inserted in the prospectus of all publicly traded mutual funds: "Past performance does not guarantee future returns." Although past performance returns should not be ignored as part of due diligence, looking ahead at general economic trends and how a firm and/or money manager makes investment decisions and their having the ability and freedom (by prospectus) to be agile and tactically react when the markets change directions is paramount.

Unlike most mutual funds and ETFs, a tactical manager can shift course and take cover in cash/money markets when the markets get rough. Most mutual funds and ETFs must remain at least 80% invested at all times according to their prospectus -- no matter how worried the fund manager might be. They typically don't have the ability to go to cash and reduce sequence of returns risk as they may like to.

Most traditional retirement accounts (IRAs, ROTHs and brokerage accounts) are invested in both stocks and bonds. Our firm combines them into a single managed bucket in one of our basic portfolios such as: Aggressive, Moderate Aggressive, Moderate, Conservative and Income and make changes whenever needed within each of those portfolio models to reduce risks and volatility while still getting good risk-adjusted returns over time – after all fees and expenses. Investment returns the investor gets to keep and enjoy.

Once the client chooses a portfolio model that best fits their risk profile for a certain account (how much risk they can really handle when markets are very rocky), our firm monitors it daily and will make any adjustments necessary to attempt to maintain the desired risk/return profile. Unlike many other investment firms, it's continuous daily oversight and management -- not set it and forget it.

So not only does the individual money manager/fund have the latitude to make changes within their portion of the model portfolio, the total portfolio model itself can be tactically altered by the firm to suit what's actually happening in the equity and fixed income markets.

That's very important - that each portfolio model as a whole can be dynamically shifted whenever needed to adjust to falling stock prices, rising interest rates, world events, etc. – all by pushing a button. This continuous portfolio management style is a bit unique in the industry.

I was with a prospective client couple last night who brought me the statement from his IRA which is being held and "managed" at one of the biggest banks in the country. The account was about $600,000 and the statement was pretty thick. There were dozens and dozens of $5,000 single bond holdings, mutual funds, ETFs and individual stocks.

They were under the false impression that their "portfolio" was being monitored every day by one of the biggest household names in the brokerage business. I told them that with all the millions of investment clients/accounts that bank has across the country, there was not likely a single portfolio that looked anything like their own.

Their situation is no different from many other small clients with their savings invested there. They just owned a collection of various investments (stuff) sold to them over the years that were deemed "suitable" for them at the time. Not a true portfolio with a purpose.

Google the difference in "suitability" vs. "fiduciary" as far as investment advice and "standard of care" goes. Their bank stock-broker operates under the "suitability standard" while investment advisory firms operate as a "fiduciary". I won't write more about it here, since there is still a "war" going on between the brokerage houses and the investment advisory business, the DOL, the SEC and the states for investor protection. The battle for retirement account protection and full disclosure is far from over. Stay tuned.

Let's get back to this couple. The reality is, that <u>nobody</u> is looking at their individual account daily, weekly or even monthly. Their advisor (like most others) is busy meeting sales quotas set by the management – bringing in new money. Everyone has to earn a living. I get that.

However, the way our firm operates, is that I am the planner. I design the plan, help clients choose the right model portfolio and/or products for them, implement the full financial, retirement plan or their Get Me to ZERO™ strategy and then continue as their financial advisor/coach – making sure the plan and investments (risk/reward) are doing what they are supposed to in relation to their goals.

But I cannot look at each clients' accounts daily. That's the real truth that too few investment professionals will admit to. They don't have the time. But it's a big plus for my clients! I do what I do best (income planning, teaching and coaching) and outsource the investing and daily account monitoring to my firm's full-time investment committee.

What happens at our SEC Registered Investment Advisory firm is that each individual money manager is looking at their own strategy's investments every day and making any adjustments necessary (much like a mutual fund manager would) -- only with more latitude to make changes. On top of that, our firm's "investment committee" is monitoring each of the total model portfolios every business day too.

Do they need to make any allocation adjustments in the percentage of holdings of any single money manager based on what's happening in the markets in a model? All models? Do they need to replace a manager that's not pulling their weight vs. their peers? Go to cash?

My firm does that daily for 19,000+ accounts across the country and it's easy since there are just a few model portfolios to watch over. Our clients benefit from that daily oversight (behind the scenes) – without my involvement. I'm busy focusing on, coaching and monitoring my client's goals. And yes, I'm also adding new clients, building new plans.

FYI: With the TRIPLE ZERO™ plans, we can only reallocate among the various index strategies on your policy anniversary once a year, so these accounts are very easy to manage. And I'm very hands-on there.

Anyway since after reading my books, many people email or call me to ask how our fee-only investment advisory firm invests our client's retirement savings? So that in a nutshell, is what we do to reduce Sequence of Returns risk as much as possible for bucket #2. That's the bucket with inherent market risk (and interest rate risk).

Of course, you may have an advisor that you're happy with or are a DIYer (Do It Yourselfer). That's great. However, bucket #2 always has sequence of returns risk – no matter who is managing the portfolio.

As I've written before, it's my long-held belief that investors should not take an ounce more risk than they need to, in order to meet their financial and retirement lifestyle goals (which usually means having a better life with less financial stress). Why take more risk than you need... to fully meet your income, lifestyle and legacy goals? Really!

Think about this for just a moment. What "potential" return goal is worth losing your sleep over and putting much of your life savings at risk for? Is it 11%, 16% or 20%. How much risk are you willing to take... and how much risk can you afford to take? We should have guardrails.

But most of us do need to take some market risk to combat inflation and meet your lifestyle goals over a 30+ year retirement. I'm not against taking market risks with "no floor" like TRIPLE ZERO™ plans. I just believe that folks should mitigate as much market risk as possible by adding tactical model portfolios with full-time daily oversight to earn more consistent returns over time with lower volatility. Anyway...

Keep in mind that bonds have risks too. They have credit risk, default risk, duration and interest rate risk. I've seen the "guaranteed" 10-year US Treasury bonds lose -10% value in a matter of months!

So let's assume you've done your work towards Get Me to ZERO™ to reduce your risk of potential tax increases and the lowering of tax brackets. You're getting prepared for what the IRS may do next. Good.

Then you reduce your sequence of returns risk in your ROTHs as much as possible (at least during the five years before you retire and during the first 5-10 years thereafter) in order to increase the likelihood of enjoying the lifestyle and financial freedom you deserve and desire. Lower your risk. Pay the IRS less. Keep more. Happy life.

I wrote earlier, if you want to take risks (bucket #2) in your Get Me to ZERO™ plan, the ROTHs are where I'd take them. I just think it's wise to try and reduce your drawdown and sequence of returns risk.

And you've already seen that the tax-free TRIPLE ZERO™ plans will give you a substantial portion of the stock market's total return including dividends (capture ratio) with the comfort of a ZERO percent floor – no market losses. With no market losses, there is no sequence of returns risk. But you can't own an IUL in a ROTH or traditional IRA.

I know that everyone wants great rates of return. Although several of my wisest professional peers feel that far too many people planning for retirement focus too much on getting the highest returns... rather than on enjoying the type of retirement life that they truly desire. Good investment returns (ROI) are important but "return on life" (ROL) is paramount since market returns can be fleeting and past returns can be completely erased in a bad recession. So, should rate of return be the main focus in your income planning process? How much of your return do you get to keep after taxes? How much risk is taken?

Imagine focusing on and measuring the results of your retirement planning in terms of how your investment "reality" is matching your lifestyle goals. Enjoying your income without worry or stress due to the ups and downs of the economy, stock markets and interest rates. What if your focus was on living... rather than on money/returns?

So for the folks that want some additional retirement savings in the Principal Protected bucket #1 (no market risk), I often look to a Fixed Index Annuity (FIA) for a <u>portion</u> of their ROTH/IRA money. Of course, you can get Principal Protection from a CD and similar savings account at a bank, but history shows CD interest rates fail to keep ahead of inflation over long periods of time. Although your bank account statement will never show a loss, if the after-tax interest rate is lower than "real-life" inflation, you will lose purchasing power.

But what you cannot do with a CD or similar Principal Protected type accounts such as T-bills and savings accounts, is to eliminate your longevity risk – either you or your spouse outliving your money.

What can do that? Principal Protected Fixed Index Annuities can play an important role in a ROTH (or traditional IRAs) for people that want either: 1) a source of guaranteed "pension-like" lifetime income without any market risk and/or 2) a very attractive alternative to bond funds without interest rate or duration risk. And if the FIA is held inside of a ROTH, of course, the income from it would be TAX-FREE.

Since the focus of this book is to help folks get to the tax-free zone during retirement, I will not spend the 30-45 pages on using FIAs here like I did in my "Retirement Income Planning" book or write about how FIAs play a role in an "income allocation plan". It's worth reading. A retirement income allocation plan creates as much of a predictable, sustainable and guaranteed income stream (pensions, Social Security, FIAs) that pays for all or most of your primary fixed monthly expenses as possible. Expenses like housing, food, insurance, utilities, etc. – what one of my clients calls his "monthly nut". Not the travel and fun expenses – but just the necessary monthly "must-pay" ones.

By the way, if you did read my Retirement Income Planning" book, you may be wondering why I didn't write much about the Get Me to ZERO™ strategy in that book. The reason is very simple. That book was written in response to readers of my "Social Security Income Planning" book contacting me from across the USA. Readers of that book bought it because they were about to retire within the next year or two and wanted information about filing for Social Security benefits. One said he was "retiring next week and wanted help right away on what to do with Social Security"! Anyway, I wrote "Retirement Income Planning" with them in mind. Most didn't have enough time to do ROTH conversions, 72(t)s or begin to contribute to a ROTH 401K. There is little "tax work" we could do for most folks within such a short time before retirement. Hopefully, you have time as well as the desire.

Back to FIAs. Some of my clients are not interested or do not think they need another guaranteed source of monthly income to add to Social Security and perhaps a pension. But... many do see the value in using an FIA as a portfolio vehicle to take the place of bonds in their portfolio. Unlike bonds, an FIA cannot go down in value due to rising interest rates. And over time, I believe their total returns will be more attractive than a bond portfolio, bond ETF or bond mutual fund.

However, many folks do like the fact that the FIA can offer a rising lifetime of guaranteed income to combat against longevity risk. Compared to a CD ladder or bond portfolio this feature can be of huge value. But this might not be appealing to you or fit with your goals.

FIAs work in a similar way to IULs in that the returns you earn are tied to a market index(s), but your money is never invested in the market (using options again) so there are no market losses possible (with lock and reset). The only way you could lose money is if you take your money out too fast and be subject to early surrender charges.

As I wrote in the "Retirement Income Planning" book, "there are only two possible doors to go through at retirement. Door #1: is that your MONEY will outlive you. Door #2: is that YOU will outlive your money! There is NO 3rd door!" Hence the attractiveness, to many people, of the guaranteed lifetime income (joint or single) options to eliminate longevity risk for these Principal Protected accounts.

Dr. Pfau holds a doctorate in Economics from Princeton University and serves as a Professor of Retirement Income in the Ph.D. program at the American College and is the co-editor of the Journal of Personal Finance. He often writes about the two fundamentally different retirement income philosophies which he calls: "probability-based" and "safety first". Each one has its own pros and cons.

Primarily choosing one belief over the other will set the overall direction and predictability of one's future income plan and lifestyle.

Those favoring "probability-based" (Risk Bucket #2) will rely on the belief that the markets will provide large enough returns over time to compensate for the occasional yet likely negative returns. They say, "why should they give up the upside?" in return for lower returns with more guarantees. However, opponents point out that this philosophy leaves folks with both sequence of return and longevity risk. This might mean outliving one's money and/or being forced to cut lifestyle.

The "safety-first" (Risk Bucket #1) mindset believes that, <u>at least the essential costs of living expenses</u> should be covered by guaranteed income from Social Security, pensions and fixed income annuities. These income sources are guaranteed and eliminate both sequence of returns risk, the risk of living too long and/or outliving your money. Lifestyle expenses "over and above" your monthly necessities and perhaps leaving a future legacy could be met with using market-based investments (bucket #2). They believe this approach is more prudent.

Now you've probably seen the TV and magazine ads from the guy who "hates annuities... and thinks you should too". He owns one of the biggest investment advisory firms in the country and is worth $3.7 BILLION (Forbes). Like me, he is a financial fiduciary. His newest commercials say that he "would rather die and go to hell than sell an annuity" and "I'll never sell an annuity". He's mostly talking about very <u>high-cost/high-risk</u> Variable Annuities (VAs) sold by stockbrokers and banks. I agree. I wouldn't sell one of those VAs either now!

But he lumps ALL annuities into one huge basket. Fixed Annuities (FAs are like a 5-10-year CD) have no fees or market risk. Accumulation FIAs have NO fees or market risk. And guaranteed lifetime income FIAs typically have a 0%-1% fee (to pay for the lifetime income guarantee) and no market risk. That 1% fee is probably similar to what he charges his small clients – with no guaranteed lifetime income, no protection from market losses/sequence risk nor locking in any past gains either.

He and his multi-millionaire clients don't need annuities to make their "monthly nut". He could lose 90% of his own assets in the stock market and still be very wealthy. With his wealth, he doesn't have longevity risk either. He could live to be age 650 and never run out of money. He's very different from you and I.

There is one other big reason why he hates annuities. He doesn't get paid on them. His fee-only firm charges his clients a fee based on the amount of money his firm manages for the client and over time, earns <u>much more</u> than any annuity agent's commission. It's a fee for "assets under management" arrangement. That's how he got to be a billionaire. In fact, he makes so much profit in quarterly fees, he'll even pay any surrender charges or early withdrawal penalties one may have in an annuity they own -- if they move those funds to his firm.

There's nothing wrong with fees. In fact, I and tens of thousands of other investment advisor representatives across the country charge fees for assets under management (and for ongoing financial planning/advice/coaching) as well. It's the fastest growing way to be compensated in the financial world (as opposed to being paid trading commissions like in the old days). Even the US government prefers fees over commissions, despite fees being much more expensive for clients over time. But what about the Principal Protected bucket?

Since he is a fiduciary like I am, and must put his client's interests before his own, I have a lot of important questions for him: "Where are you going to put your client's money that is protected from all market risk and can still earn respectable returns, (and tax-deferred for non-IRAs)? What investments will your non-millionaire clients (minimum investment with him is $500,000 according to his ads) place money in that they can't afford to, or do not want to lose?"

"What investments do you offer to take sequence of returns risk off of the table?" "Which of your investments totally eliminate longevity risk?" "Do your stocks and bonds offer any LTC potential protection?"

In my mind, an advisor cannot truly be a fiduciary and have 100% of the clients' best interest at heart, if one advises every single person that ALL annuities have no place in any income portfolio. In fact, the best academic research clearly shows that blanket statement... is false.

Dr. Wade Pfau told the Wall Street Journal: "Use annuities instead of bonds. Pairing... an annuity—with stocks, retirees can generate income more safely and reliably than if they use bonds for that piece of their portfolio". He went on to say: "There is no need for retirees to hold bonds. Instead, annuities, with their promise of income for life, act like super bonds with no maturity dates." I've seen client FIAs credit 10% or more in some recent years. Not normal, but it happens.

In May 2018, research published by highly-regarded asset-allocation firm Ibbotson Associates is "championing FIAs as a bond alternative for investors approaching retirement". What a compelling retirement income portfolio combination – having part of your savings get the upside of the stock market (perhaps managed tactically with daily oversight) along with part invested in an FIA which avoids market losses and interest rate risk with contractual lifetime (and perhaps rising) income guarantees (joint or single life) replacing the bonds.

All annuity income guarantees operate from the basis of math and actuarial science. It's actuarial science that academic researchers refer to as "mortality credits". And no place to invest, other than insurance, can provide mortality credits. It's the mathematical science of risk-pooling. It's something that only an insurance company can do.

If you own life insurance, you already have mortality credits working on your behalf. How else can a term life insurance company pay $1,000,000 death benefit on a 27-year-old male who had only made one $35 monthly premium and then gets killed by a drunk driver? But the death benefit will get paid! The insurer's actuaries know that most 27-year old's will live for many decades beyond their term policy and prices this into the required premiums. They also know that most people let them lapse years before the term ends.

Here's something to think about. Many folks ask me, what is the internal rate of return on a guaranteed lifetime income annuity? I answer them by saying, "what do you want it to be?" The truth is, the insurance company does NOT set that rate of return itself.

You see, YOU (and perhaps your spouse) determine what the true internal rate of return on your FIA will be – by how long one or both of you will live. That's mortality credits providing guaranteed retirement income "alpha" that you cannot get anywhere else.

Mortality credits are based on your age and gender. If you and/or your spouse are very healthy, the likelihood is that one/both of you will live longer than the average life expectancy. To get an even better return – just live longer. Beat the CSO tables. I'm not kidding!

It is important to note that any contractual "guarantee" issued by an insurance company (life insurance and annuities) is solely backed by the financial strength and the "claims paying ability" of the insurer. Throughout this book, when I refer to guarantees of a FIA or IUL, I am referring to the contractual guarantee as described above. Having written that regulatory disclaimer, I almost always recommend insurers with very high financial ratings ("A" or "A+" rated from AM Best) that have an unbroken history of making good on their promises (contractual guarantees) for many decades.

Before I continue, let me write a few words about all financial products and services. ALL financial products are just "tools". Each financial product: stocks, bonds, mutual funds, ETF's, real estate, limited partnerships, SPIAs, fixed annuities, reverse mortgages, IULs, whole life policies, CDs, etc., have a specific purpose just like tools do.

You use a screwdriver to screw two materials together. You do not use it to put a nail in the wall. A saw is great tool to cut a piece of wood, but it makes an awful hammer. The same with golf clubs. Each golf club serves a specific function. You get the idea. Each type of financial product has a unique function. Every financial product has its own purpose (and pros... and cons too). When used properly it will do the job well. When used inappropriately – you've got a problem.

Most FIAs are best suited to provide either a contractually guaranteed lifetime (single or joint) income without market risk... or be a good bond alternative and act as a portfolio "ballast" to stocks (exactly what the March 2014 Wall Street Journal article argues) with average annual returns of maybe 4%, 5% or perhaps 6%.

An FIA is not meant to compete with the high potential returns of real estate, stocks, ETFs or equity mutual funds. FIAs belong in bucket #1 with CDs or T-bills – with much higher potential long-term returns.

Anyway, I'm not here to push FIAs (or IULs or daily tactical portfolio management). This book is all about the Get Me to ZERO™ strategy. Some folks can do all of it with just ROTHs invested only in the stock and bond markets plus using the standard deduction. Or you may need to add a TRIPLE ZERO™ plan and implement some of the other four strategies as well to get you there – or get as close as possible.

How much risk do you want, or can you afford to take? As stated above, there are basically two buckets you can put your ROTH and other savings into. A bucket with no market risk (#1) or a bucket with "a little... up to a lot of market and interest rate risk" (#2).

If you and/or your spouse live about 30 years in retirement, you'll likely face 4-6 recessions during those years. And one could be lurking within five years or so before you retire. Thinking about real risk (losses) and potential reward (gains) is an important consideration.

Most of my own clients use both risk buckets in the way I've described above. But of course, you can handle this any way that you'd like. The FIA is just another tool that's available for you to reach your retirement goals. That's all, just another club in your golf bag.

3 Half-Truths and Misconceptions

As promised earlier in the book, I'd like to address what you'll likely find when you google IULs. Of course, you can believe what you'd like. I'm just here to tell you that if I believed any of that misinformation on the internet, I would not own five IULs -- with those being 100% of my own retirement plan. Not what I'd recommend to most folks, but that's what's best for me and my goals in my own personal situation.

Before I get started, let me pronounce that an IUL is not a guaranteed product. Of course, there are some guaranteed elements in the policy. But just like there are not any return guarantees in your 401K or ROTH, there are no guarantees related to interest crediting in your IUL. As previously stated, you are guaranteed to never lose money because of market declines and there is real value in that. If you are seeking a guaranteed product, don't purchase an IUL. And keep in mind that the dividend in a whole life policy is not guaranteed, and without it, that policy doesn't look as good, as <u>with</u> the dividends.

If you happen to work with any life agent that says something like, "All you have to do is put in "X dollars for Y years and then you are <u>guaranteed</u> to be able to pull out Z dollars of tax-free cash-flow", then run like hell away from him/her. It's likely but not guaranteed.

They should be saying something like, "I know one thing for sure. This illustration is wrong. Reality is not going to look exactly like this since we know that you are not going to get 7% returns every single year for the next 40-60 years. This illustration shows you putting in "X dollars for Y years and then taking out Z dollars of tax-free cash-flow using a 7% AVG. return every year – no zeros, no double-digit returns".

Although, based on the past 17-year history of IULs, we'll likely average about 7% returns over time (perhaps as much as 7.75% or 8%). There will be years when the market tanks and we get the 0% floor that year. (Thank goodness for that protection.) And there will be years where we'll hit the cap on some index strategies. And some years, we'll get nearly all the index's gain (over the spread) and earn 20% or more. But we'll never ever get exactly 7% each and every year.

1) Insurance Costs and Policy Expenses are high. Yes, there are costs taken out of your premiums to pay for the death benefit and all other costs associated with the life insurance policy. There is no getting around that. So, this is a half-truth. But let's examine the other half.

First of all, your agent should show you exactly where each dollar of your policy expenses is going. They can do that when they run an illustration. Most do not. What you'll see is these costs are very high during the early years (making the first 10-15 years of the policy illustration look awful). In the early years, your IRRs are not attractive at all due to the bulk of the policy expenses are front-loaded.

But as I alluded to earlier in the book (pages 105-107), a maximum funded TRIPLE ZERO™ plan that is designed to be right under the MEC-line could have cumulative tax-free IRRs over 25, 35 and more years of perhaps 6.5%, 7% or higher, since the expenses drop to a dribble the longer the policy is in-force. So, the good-half of this half-truth, is that over time, an IUL will likely have lower cumulative annual costs (less than 0.8%) than a professionally managed brokerage account or ROTH. And you do get something for those costs – a tax-free death benefit!

2) Policy costs are not guaranteed. It's possible that they could go

up. This is a truth, but there is more to the story. That cannot happen with whole life contracts because the costs are at the absolute highest level from the starting date. And if the board of the whole life insurer wants to reduce those costs in any year (most years) for policyholders, they can declare a "dividend". That's not a dividend like a stock would give to shareholders (which is taxable), but legally a return of excess premium (not taxed since you're only getting your own money back).

The "Guaranteed Page" of the IUL illustration shows you the worst-case scenario. The worst-case scenario could only happen if BOTH: 1) you get zero % returns for each of the next 30 years and 2) the day you get your new policy, the insurer informs you they have raised the policy and/or mortality costs to the highest allowed by the contract.

The guaranteed page also assumes that you do nothing about it. You just stick your head in the sand and watch your policy go to pieces. Would you do nothing at all if you got a letter about rising policy costs... or the market was going down (and crediting zero % returns) for year after year after year? Come on. Nobody is that stupid.

First of all, none of the carriers that I use have ever raised policy expenses for existing contracts. But they do have that right. Second of all, many agents do not even know that there is something that can be done to fix this. But the guaranteed page of the illustration assumes you and your agent do nothing at all for 10-20 years. Not very likely.

If the markets went down for four or five years in a row, your 401K would likely be in much worse shape than the IUL. But TRIPLE ZERO™ plans also have fixed accounts (like a 1-year CD) that were paying 4%-5% -- even during the last recession/recovery. You could move all or part of your accumulated value out of the indexes and into this account on any policy anniversary instead of doing nothing. And of course, you could do a 1035 tax-free exchange to a new IUL or annuity if you just wanted out. But you would do something!

3) Caps, Spreads and Participation Rates could change. This is also true, but the huge misconception here is that the insurer benefits by reducing them. As discussed earlier, IULs use options to get upside market potential with the downside protection of a 0% floor. The two reasons those things could (and likely will) go <u>both</u> up and down over time is: 1) the cost of options (the higher the market's volatility, the more options tend to cost) and 2) interest rate changes in the insurers' portfolio of bonds. Insurers are agnostic whether you put your funds in the fixed account or in one or more of the indexes. They do not profit by lowering caps, spreads or participation rates.

My clients and I have seen small changes in caps in both directions over the years from the top insurers -- who worry about market-share and keeping agents wanting to recommend their policies rather than those of the competition. Generally, the caps, etc., go up and down slowly across most IUL insurers at roughly similar time frames due to the economy as a whole and the competitive nature of the business.

By the way, the "dividends" of whole life insurance policies can be affected by changes in interest rates and expenses. So are banks and the interest rates they decide to pay you on CDs and savings accounts.

TRIPLE ZERO™ Checklist

There are some 118 IUL policies from about 3 dozen insurers. Before we end this discussion of TRIPLE ZERO™ plans as they relate to the Get Me to ZERO™ goal, I'd like to share a checklist of what I consider to be non-negotiable features of an IUL policy -- should you feel that owning one will help you pay as little income taxes in retirement as possible.

#1) Financial Strength of the Insurance Company. In my opinion, the company should have an "A" rating from AM Best. An "A+" rating is even better. I also like to see the insurer have at least 10-12 years of offering IUL plans, so we can judge their history with the product. And what percentage of total life insurance sales do their IULs represent?

2) Multiple Index Strategies Available. Long ago, the annual point to point S&P 500 index was the only strategy most TRIPLE ZERO™ plans offered. But having 3-5 indexes (S&P 500 and others) and/or strategies with attractive spreads and participation rates on those indexes (to take advantage when markets have large gains) are even better.

3) Loan Options. In my own TRIPLE ZERO™ policies, I have both the "wash loan" and "participating loan" options (different insurers name them differently). The <u>guaranteed</u> wash loan cost should be less than 0.5% and as close to 0% as possible – at least after the 6th year. And the participating loan option should have a <u>guaranteed</u> loan rate of 5%-6%. If it "floats" with the Moody's Bond Index (or similar), the rate may be lower when interest rates are low like from 2009-2017... BUT it should be firmly <u>capped</u> at no more than 6% (when rates go high).

Not only are both loan options available in all my policies, but I can freely change from one type to the other on any policy anniversary. That gives me great flexibility and the best of both worlds. And this is vital to optimize the future cash-flow for Get Me to ZERO™ planning.

4) The policy illustration must show both projected expenses and Internal Rates of Returns (IRRs) so these are not hidden. If the agent will not do this, then find another agent who will. And ask the agent what plan he/she has if the insurer raises these costs for any reason?

5) Daily or Weekly Sweeps. Premium dollars arrive at insurers every business day. The best IULs take that premium and buy options every day or at least weekly. It's less advantageous to an IUL owner to have that money sitting around for a month or quarter waiting to get returns that are linked to the markets. A daily or weekly option sweep also indicates the level of IUL premium volume an insurer gets and perhaps their long-term commitment to the IUL space.

6) Over-loan Protection. Most good IUL policies will have this today. This provision protects the policyholder from themselves. Taking too

much money out of your policy through policy loans ("more" than is justified by the cash accumulation inside your policy) can cause a policy to lapse. Should a policy lapse (and not payoff outstanding loans and interest through the death benefit), all previous distributions would be taxable. That would not be a good thing, to say the least. The over-loan provision can protect you from this happening at all.

Hopefully, you and your agent will monitor the level of distributions taken compared to policy performance – just like you would do with an IRA and all other accounts -- so you don't run ever out of money.

Throughout this whole book, we've discussed using multiple strategies to pay as little taxes in retirement as possible and potentially reduce other risks like sequence of returns risk. I'd like to assume that readers would be just as vigilant in monitoring ALL aspects of your retirement income plan (returns, risk, expenses, etc.) on an ongoing basis.

7) Chronic Illness Provisions. As I stated earlier in the book, many agents oversell a "free" LTC benefit when the TRIPLE ZERO™ plan is built, funded and meant to provide tax-free retirement cash-flow. Depending upon when an LTC need might occur, this provision could be very valuable (if you need it in the early policy years) or not worth very much at all when the cash value and death benefit amounts are pretty similar and/or you are already taking distributions from the policy. But I would put this "free" benefit on the shopping list too!

8) Even with a TRIPLE ZERO™ plan that includes all the above, unless it is designed properly and fully-funded (this part is up to you), I would not buy it. There are many ways to build an IUL. Some designs benefit the agent more than the policyholder. It's usually due to their not being properly trained (or trained by a selfish agent) that could cause this to happen. But sometimes it's simply an agent's plain greed.

An IUL "pro" can tell in 3 minutes of looking at any policy illustration if the agent designed the policy for his/her own benefit... or for yours.

Some Get Me to ZERO™ Questions... Answered

What if tax rates don't go up and/or tax brackets/deductions are not changed for the worse in the next 10-20 years?

Good question. With all of our country's un-funded obligations plus $22 Trillion of actual debt, do you really think that tax rates, brackets and deductions will be <u>lowered</u> for you in the future? If so, then these strategies, at least from a tax standpoint, won't make sense for you.

Tax rates don't have to double as David Walker suggests they must for your taking action to bear fruit. If tax rates (and other similar IRS tax levers) just move against you by 1%, then contributing to ROTHs, converting to ROTHs, 72(t)s, etc., will have been a wise tax decision. That's on top of trying to avoid taxation on your Social Security, avoiding RMDs plus all of the other non-tax benefits described in this book. If tax rates, etc. rise by just 5%... you've hit a home run.

Can Congress change the tax laws for TRIPLE ZERO™ plans?

Yes, they can. In fact, they have done so three times during the 1980's (TAMRA, DEFRA and TEFRA). However, in each of those cases, they grandfathered the better previous tax treatment to all existing life insurance contracts (yes - it was even better back then). Should they make changes once again, I'm betting that history will repeat itself and my own life policies will be grandfathered like before. Members of Congress own these types of life policies too!

Truth be told, they could change the rules on ROTHs too. Congress could even eliminate the IRS and "income taxes" altogether and replace them with a huge "sales tax" on every product or service we buy. The more you spend, the more taxes you pay. Who knows?

But I believe one must plan based on the present tax laws – rather than not doing any planning at all, because we don't know what a

Congress and a President will do 10, 15, or 30 years from now. That's the only prudent course of action. Does that make sense to you?

Would it be beneficial to own more than one TRIPLE ZERO™ plan?

Well, that depends on many factors. I didn't start out with five policies. I bought one with what annual amount I wanted to contribute to it. Then, I was able to contribute more (but the MEC limits would not allow me to add it to the 1st policy) so I applied for the next policy. And so on. I'd like to do one more (perhaps Catapult?), but we'll see.

Sometimes it makes sense to have a policy on each spouse since the other appreciates the death benefit as well as the living benefits (tax-free cash-flow, the Private Reserve, potential LTC benefits, etc.).

I also have clients (including myself) that like to use more than one insurer because of the different index strategies each one offers. I like index diversification (with FIAs too) the same as I like investment portfolio diversification. But if someone just wanted to put $500 a month into a TRIPLE ZERO™ plan, I'd suggest they use just one policy.

Are retirement plans like Traditional IRAs, ROTHs, 401Ks, and TRIPLE ZERO™ plans protected from creditors?

In this lawsuit happy society we live in, creditor protection is important! First of all, I'm not an attorney (nor do I play one on TV). The following is my understanding. Rather than debt issues, the legal issue my clients worry about most is a civil lawsuit (teenager's driving accident, etc.). And business owners are more worried than most.

Retirement plans at work (ERISA plan like 401Ks, etc.) have the most creditor protections. Typically, the only people who can get a piece of your 401K savings while it's inside your plan at work is: 1) the IRS and 2) an ex-spouse as part of a divorce decree. Other than that, the 401K creditor protection is virtually impenetrable to most creditors.

If you rollover those 401K funds to an IRA, it can start to get a little more complicated, since there are 2 basic types of creditor protection; 1) creditor protection in bankruptcy and 2) creditor protection in any type of non-bankruptcy event (civil lawsuit). Think O.J. Simpson.

As to creditor protection in a bankruptcy, in 2005 a federal law provided your retirement account with strong bankruptcy protection. Under that law, 401K and other ERISA plans (work-based) funds and pensions, were given unlimited protection in bankruptcy proceedings. And if you roll that money over to your IRA, the unlimited protection in bankruptcy proceedings will follow right along with it.

As to non-bankruptcy creditor protection scenarios (lawsuits), while the unlimited bankruptcy protection those funds had inside the 401K follows those dollars in a rollover to an IRA, the creditor protection in non-bankruptcy situations may not. It depends where you live.

When 401K funds are rolled over to an IRA, the non-bankruptcy creditor protection will be determined by your state's laws. According to IRA expert and CPA Ed Slott, "In some states, that protection will be roughly equivalent to the protection the funds had while they were in your 401K. In other states, your protection could be much weaker." And believe it or not, to complicate matters even more, some states actually provide traditional IRAs and Roth IRAs with different levels of creditor protection!

Contributary IRAs have federal protection in bankruptcy proceedings, (limited to $1,283,025). In non-bankruptcy situations, only state law applies to both ROTHs and traditional IRAs. And the IRS can always levy your IRA too.

TRIPLE ZERO™ plans: The cash accumulation and/or death benefit in life insurance policies are partially or fully protected from most creditors and lawsuits in most states (100% creditor protected in AL, FL, KY, IL, IN, MD, MO, NC, NJ, NY, TN, TX and some other states).

By the way, your taxable brokerage accounts, bank accounts, real estate (many primary residences, vacation homes and investment properties) and most other assets are not generally protected from bankruptcy, civil court judgments and non-bankruptcy cases. The rules vary by state so please consult an attorney.

Although an "umbrella" insurance policy will not protect you against many creditor issues, it will help protect your assets from lawsuits due to and arising from (and above and beyond) your car and homeowner's insurance limits. I always recommend you get at least $1 million of umbrella coverage. I have a $2 million umbrella policy.

What if I'm not healthy enough to get a good rate or even qualify for any life insurance?

That happens more than most people think. When this occurs, we use a "surrogate" insured. You would be the owner of the policy and control all the cash accumulation and designate the beneficiaries, etc. But the death benefit would be paid on someone else's passing away.

There must be some insurable interest (a real reason to do this) in order for you to own a policy on another person's life. Typically, this would be a spouse, child, parent or business partner.

I can buy stocks, bonds and mutual funds on my own. Why would I need an insurance agent (who gets a commission) to own a TRIPLE ZERO™ plan?

You can buy term life insurance online (although you typically still must take some type of health exam if the policy's death benefit is over $100,000). Even though that's pretty simple to do, you do not avoid a commission being paid. The owner of the website must be a licensed agent and is selling the same exact policies as the guy does sitting at your kitchen table. The policies online are exactly the same as from an agent. A commission gets paid in either case. The consumer does not save a dime by foregoing a live person's help and advice.

To my knowledge, there is no way to buy an IUL online. Perhaps there is or will be at some point. But as you probably understand after reading this book, there is a lot more to designing and positioning this product than just saying you want a $1,000,000, 20-year term policy and want to know the monthly premium.

Even most insurance agents don't have a clue. And if (when?) you can buy an IUL online, just like with any other insurance policy (car, renters, home, etc.) a commission will be paid to the owner of the website (who must be a licensed agent in the state you reside).

The commission does not add to your premium, so I see no benefit to not getting the most experienced, hands-on professional help you can for the same exact premium dollars contributed.

What if I really like the attributes of a TRIPLE ZERO™ plan, but I can't afford to contribute much more than to my ROTH right now?

Great job on contributing to a ROTH. You have begun the journey to Get Me to ZERO™. Do you have a ROTH 401K option too? Many times, I can help folks "find the money" to start your IUL now. There are 4 major "money moves" we use to be more efficient in your financial life and fund a sizable TRIPLE ZERO™ - without changing your lifestyle.

But if not, if you can afford to invest at least $500/month to a TRIPLE ZERO™ plan within 3, 5 or 10 years (depending upon your age, sex and health), you might consider getting a "convertible term" policy until you can afford your IUL. A convertible term policy gives you immediate death benefit coverage and locks in your insurability to upgrade to an IUL within a certain number of years (sometimes up to 30 years). Some insurers will even give you some credit on your previously-paid term premiums. But the convertible term policy will typically only allow you to convert to an IUL product from that same insurance company. So, you want to make sure that you buy the term insurance from a company that you want to own eventually your IUL.

Mark, my husband and I make over $850,000 a year combined. Does it make sense for us to <u>NOT</u> take every deduction we can get today?

There are many factors to consider. You are currently in the highest tax bracket with marginal rates of 37% plus a 3.8% surtax on any investment income from taxable accounts. Historically, those in the highest tax brackets will remain in the highest brackets (the rich get richer). The top 1% of earners pay 40% of total personal income taxes!

If you think your taxes in retirement will be lower, then take your full deductions in the traditional 401K now. If not, and a ROTH 401K option is available to you, I'd do that. In either case, hopefully you are saving a ton of money outside of your qualified plans for your future. In a taxable account you'll get 1099's and pay taxes every year.

Here's a perfect place for a TRIPLE ZERO™. Unlimited contributions, no income restrictions, no 1099's and tax-free access (Private Reserve) and retirement cash-flow with no market risk. Perhaps even the Catapult plan. I'd need more info regarding your situation and goals.

And finally, why hasn't my CPA told me about Get Me to ZERO™?

There are almost as many reasons for that as there are CPAs, Enrolled Agents (EAs) and other tax professionals. But for me, it boils down to two main factors. Look at the logo on my business card (page 195).

First of all, in my experience, I've found that most CPAs were never trained on cash-value life insurance (and all annuities for that matter). Next month I'll be hosting another 4-hour Continuing Education class (CPE credits) for CPAs. Based on their past course evaluations, they love it. The difference in their knowledge on this subject matter from the beginning of the class... to the end, is like "night and day". And we've only scratched the surface of these two subjects in four hours.

Let alone teaching any other advanced financial planning such as

Social Security strategies, ROTH conversions, 72(t)s, MIS's, reverse mortgages, QCDs, etc. No more than I could charge somebody to do tax returns after a 4-hour course. We each have our areas of expertise.

The other main factor that I've found with CPAs is many of them are just overwhelmed with their primary duties of tax preparation, audits and compliance paperwork – especially during tax season. Many of these dedicated tax professionals are working 12-15-hour days, six or seven days a week during peak tax season. Not a great work/life balance. They are paid to produce timely, accurate tax returns as well as make sure they get you all of your rightful current deductions.

While all are experts at recording tax history, many view their job as saving you taxes today – rather than preparing you for the potential of higher future taxes/avoiding RMDs/taxation of SS, etc. Most folks want instant gratification. They say, "Save me taxes TODAY"!

Few CPAs are compensated to provide longer-term proactive tax planning. Many would like to do this and provide more extensive planning services for those clients who could benefit. One of my business initiatives is helping CPAs "shine", by extending their relationship with their clients through a much deeper-dive into their present financial circumstances and future goals with comprehensive financial and tax planning. I'll even use outside specialists when appropriate.

To accomplish this initiative, I'm affiliated with two organizations that help CPAs change their practice. To do more of the work that they like to do and find most interesting (planning and advice) and perhaps less of the more mundane functions someone else in the office could do.

Our CPA Team-Based Model is a solution-focused planning platform to empower them to proactively increase their value to their clients with comprehensive financial, business and tax advice. Holistic strategies and solutions based on the client's goals with the CPA (quarterback) and advisor working together on an encompassing plan to meet them.

The darker part of the logo represents the client and the other two parts are the CPA and advisor working for a win-win-win. The client gets more proactive and advanced planning, the CPA gets more tax interesting work (overall wealth management oversight) and is well compensated for it and the advisor earns a new long-term happy client. And this planning would go far beyond the Get Me to ZERO™ strategy. There's much that can be done to make their financial life better – particularly for successful business owners and the affluent.

So yes, more and more CPAs will understand and recommend this planning -- especially for those clients who fear future tax increases.

Final Thoughts

It is my sincere hope that you have not only learned a lot by reading this book but enjoyed it as well. If so, please let your friends know about it. I'm passionate about teaching all types of financial concepts.

If you believe taxes are going to cost you much more in the years to come (rising tax rates, changing brackets and fewer deductions, etc.) based on the reality of our country's financial circumstances and huge obligations to its' citizens, this is a good pathway to position yourself to pay the lowest taxes allowed by law. And the other benefits of this planning, such as reducing risks (sequence of returns, longevity, LTC and inflation) and taking advantage of opportunities (Private Reserve, etc.) can add real value to both your present and long-term future.

Beyond financial considerations, the real point and endgame of all financial planning is to enjoy a happier and more secure life. Saving taxes and reducing market risks can and will help financially. But it's not the money... but what the money can do for you and your family!

With your permission, I'll use this last page for a "commercial". If what you've read in this book resonates with where you find yourself financially today and where you'd like to be in the future, contact me.

Most of my current clients are readers of my books. Folks from across the country who read new and interesting strategies and perspectives, that have reached out to me for further information.

In my "Retirement Income Planning" book, I wrote about designing a retirement income "road map" for my clients who are within a few years of retirement – or are already retired. They typically don't have enough years to implement a full Get Me to ZERO™ plan of action.

If you have at least 5 to 30+ years to make your ROTH contributions, implement ROTH conversions, use a 72(t) and/or find other money to fund a TRIPLE ZERO™ plan, you would likely want me to overlay as many of the seven Get Me to ZERO™ strategies in your "future income road map" as possible, to minimize your taxation during retirement. It's always fun help folks save taxes, reduce risk and have a better life.

I invite readers who are interested in learning more about my planning services and/or using these strategies to reduce their future taxes on Social Security, have better access and control over their retirement funds, avoid RMDs, etc... to reach out to me. The less you pay the IRS, the more you keep and get to enjoy. It's pretty simple.

There is no cost nor any obligation to have a 30-minute introductory conversation with me about my planning process and philosophy or if you're just looking for a professional 2nd opinion. As a fiduciary (putting your interests first), I work on a collaborative basis. I'll listen to your vision of your future. It's your retirement and money, not mine. I'll work with you to help you attain your own goals using the financial tools and services that you feel most comfortable with.

I hope to hear from you!   All the best... Mark

About the Author: Mark J. Orr, CFP® RICP®

770-777-8309 Office
morr@RetirementWealthAdvisors.com
Instagram: @getmetozero   facebook.com/get-me-to-zero
www.SmartFinancialPlanning.com
12600 Deerfield Parkway Suite #100   Alpharetta, GA 30004

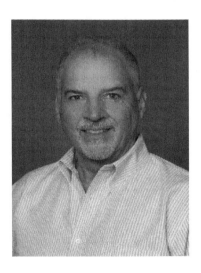

Mark has been a practicing Certified Financial Planner™ since 2000. Certified Financial Planners are held to the strictest ethical and fiduciary standards. He has also earned the year-long Retirement Income Certified Professional® (RICP®) designation. Since 1997, he has held life, health and the Series 7 Securities license (no longer held) and became a Registered Investment Advisor soon thereafter owning his own fee-based firm from 1999-2016.

He is now an Investment Advisor Representative with Retirement Wealth Advisors where FormulaFolios manages his clients' stock and bond market-based investments – (bucket #2) using tactical wealth money managers. These fee-only accounts are allocated into portfolios based on a client's risk tolerance, tax situation, time horizon, and their income and legacy goals. These money managers focus first on minimizing sequence of returns risk (and drawdown) while capturing as much of the market's upside as possible with daily oversight from our full-time professional investment committee.

He is also the author two other books: 1) "Social Security Income Planning: The Baby Boomers' 2019 Guide to Maximize Your Retirement Benefits" and 2) "Retirement Income Planning" as well as several white papers and eBooks. He has led dozens of public seminars on various financial planning and retirement topics. He's been quoted twice in the USA TODAY as well as being a guest on several morning radio shows across the country.

Prior to the financial services business, Mark spent the early part of his career in the luxury resort real estate development and marketing industry — managing $100 million of sales in Europe over a 7-year period. That was back when that was "real" money -- lol! After that, he owned a few franchises and then sold those businesses.

He is a current and three-time past board member of his Rotary Club and continues to be active in community service through the Rotary Club. On a personal note, Mark and Norma live in Alpharetta, Georgia and love to travel — especially to warm sandy beaches. Staying in good shape is very important to him and he enjoys good red wine. Finally, he is the awfully proud father of three grown children (Megan, Marina and Michael) and four wonderful grandchildren (so far).

Acknowledgments and Disclosures

I'd like to thank long-time mentors', colleagues and great friends of the EAGLE TEAM and my 20 Group. I am so fortunate to be a part of your growing organization and our fantastic study group. And Don Blanton for teaching me so much over time as well as for his powerful software.

The opinions and views written in this book are those of the author and do not necessarily represent those of any person, organization or firm that I have been associated with (either in the past, are currently or may be in the future). This book is intended to provide general information only and that no individual professional financial advice is offered herein. The author is not a CPA or certified tax professional. The author is not an attorney nor is he a licensed mortgage broker. Neither the author nor publisher intend to or is rendering any professional services including but not limited to: tax advice, investment advice, insurance advice, legal advice or mortgage advice. This book, nor any words written within its pages should be interpreted as giving any such personal advice and should not be relied upon.

Thank you again for your purchase and for reading my book. I hope that it has opened your eyes to the many wonderful TAX-FREE possibilities ahead for you during your retirement!

Made in the USA
Columbia, SC
15 April 2019